MW01681050

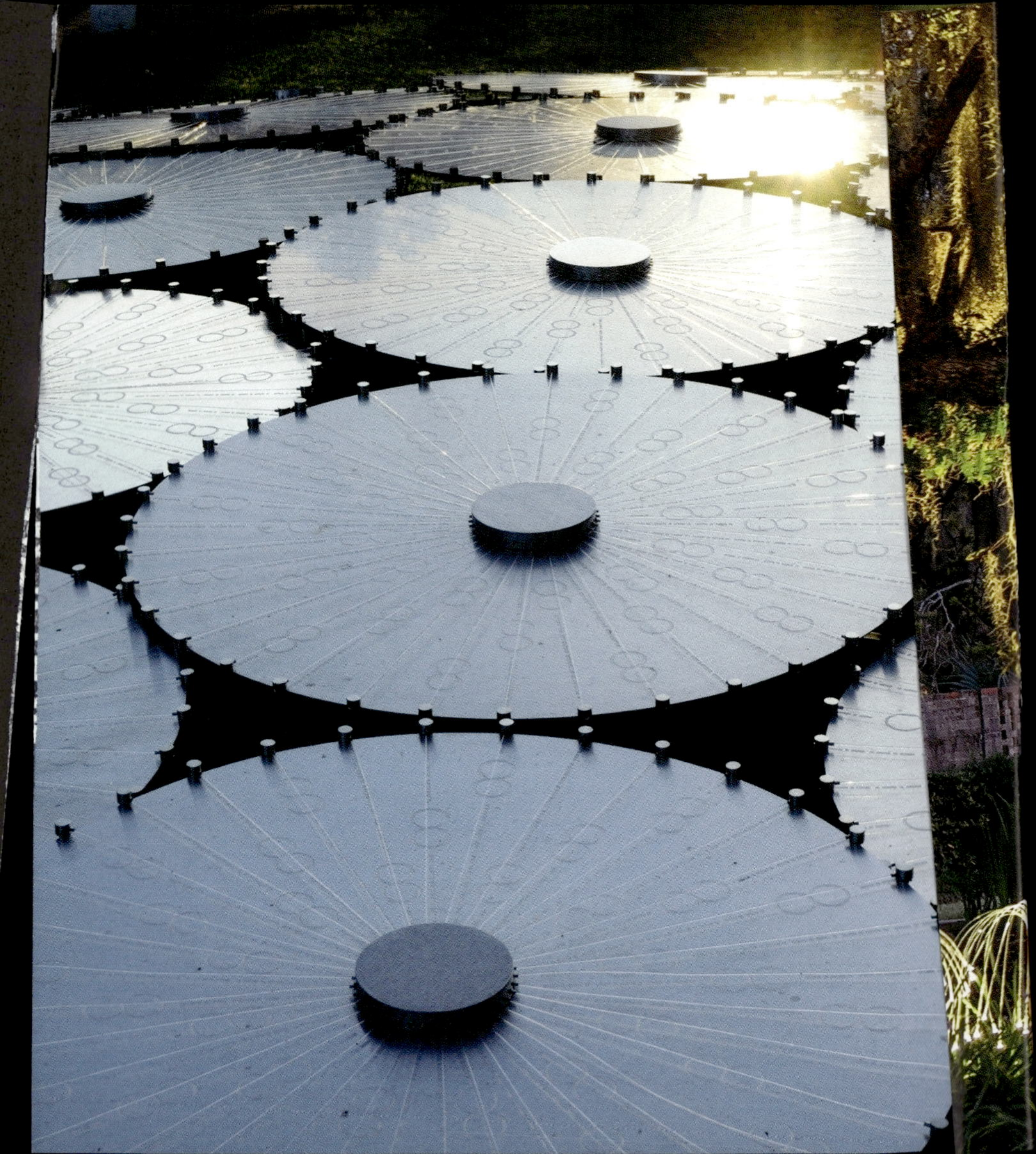

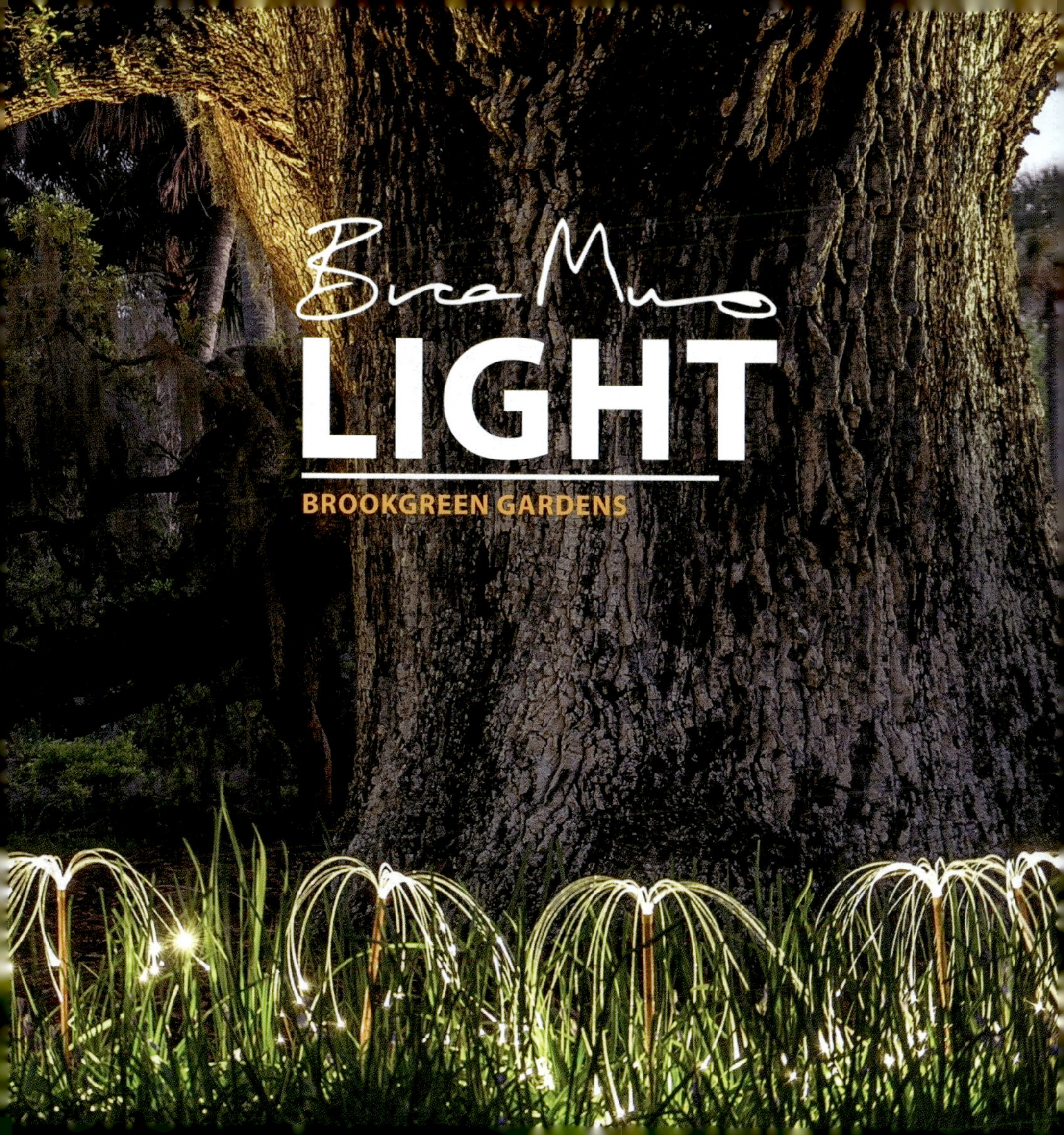
Bruce Munro
LIGHT
BROOKGREEN GARDENS

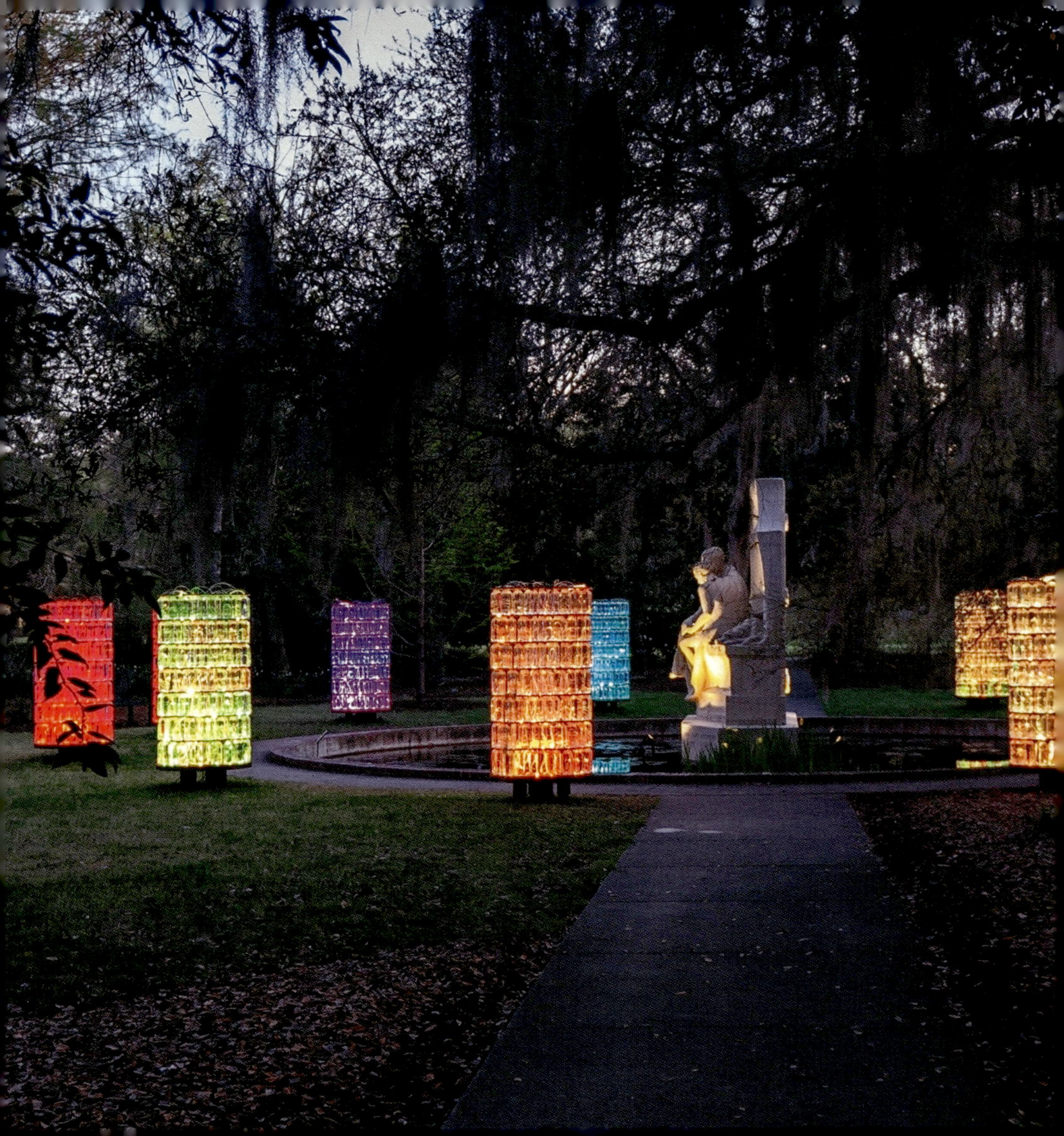

Bruce Munro at BROOKGREEN SOUTHERN LIGHT

Upon the founding of Brookgreen Gardens, Archer Huntington described its purpose as "a quiet joining of hands between science and art." The first public sculpture garden in America, Brookgreen Gardens has developed, refined, and excelled in the outdoor exhibition of art. We are excited that Bruce Munro was inspired by our permanent collection of art and botanical gardens as the canvas to create *Bruce Munro at Brookgreen: Southern Light*.

The year 2021 will mark the ninetieth year since Brookgreen's founding, and our wish is that this exhibit will introduce the Gardens to new guests and engage the public in this unique experience. Brookgreen strives to educate a diverse audience about nature, history, and art. The creative spark for this exhibit is largely found in nature and our unique Southern landscape. We hope you immerse yourself in this exhibit and carry the memories of your visit into the future.

On behalf of our entire staff and volunteer team, we are honored to welcome you to *Bruce Munro at Brookgreen: Southern Light*.

—Page Kiniry, President and CEO, Brookgreen Gardens

Pp. 1–7; Brookgreen Gardens, South Carolina, USA, 2020.

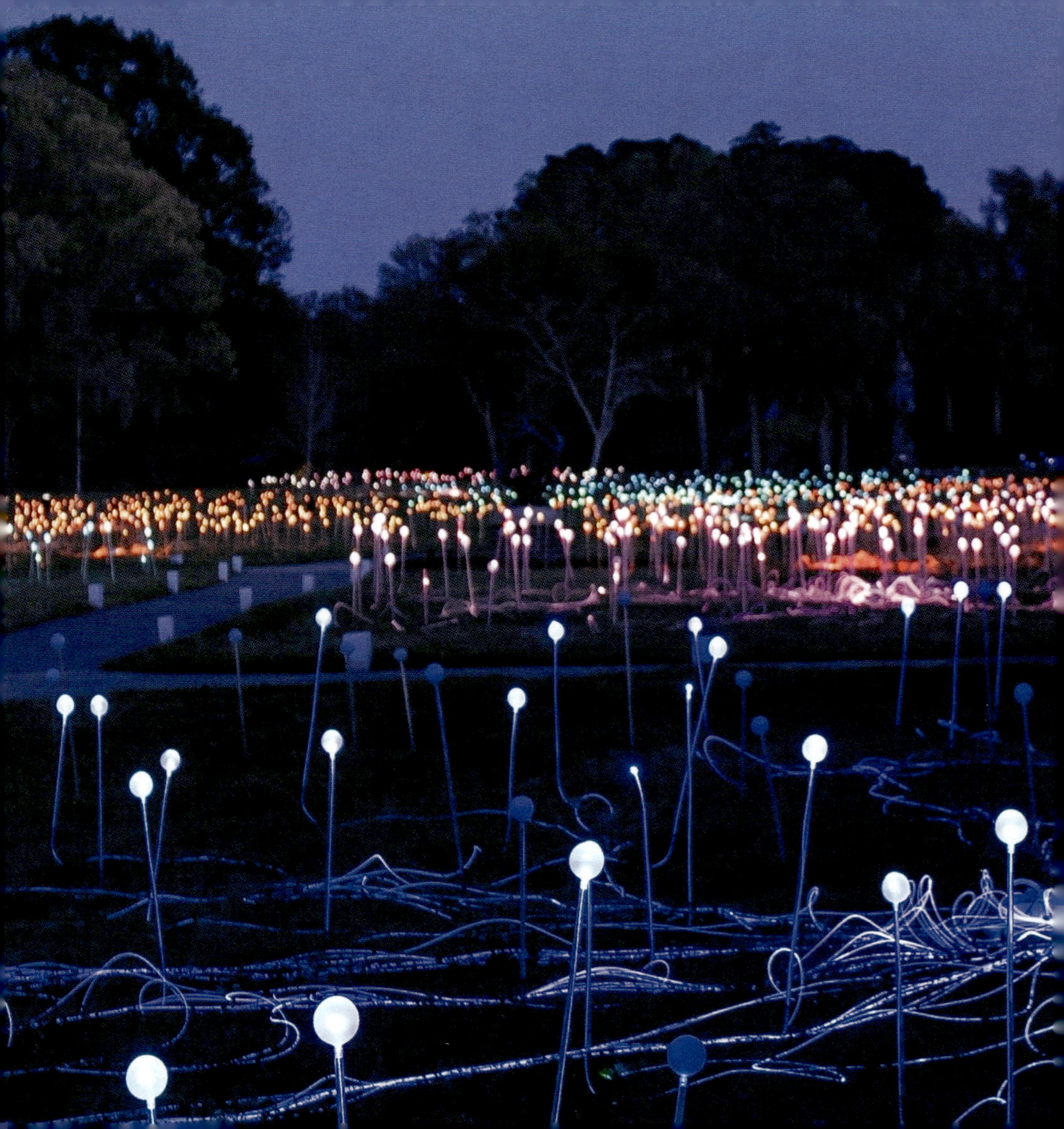

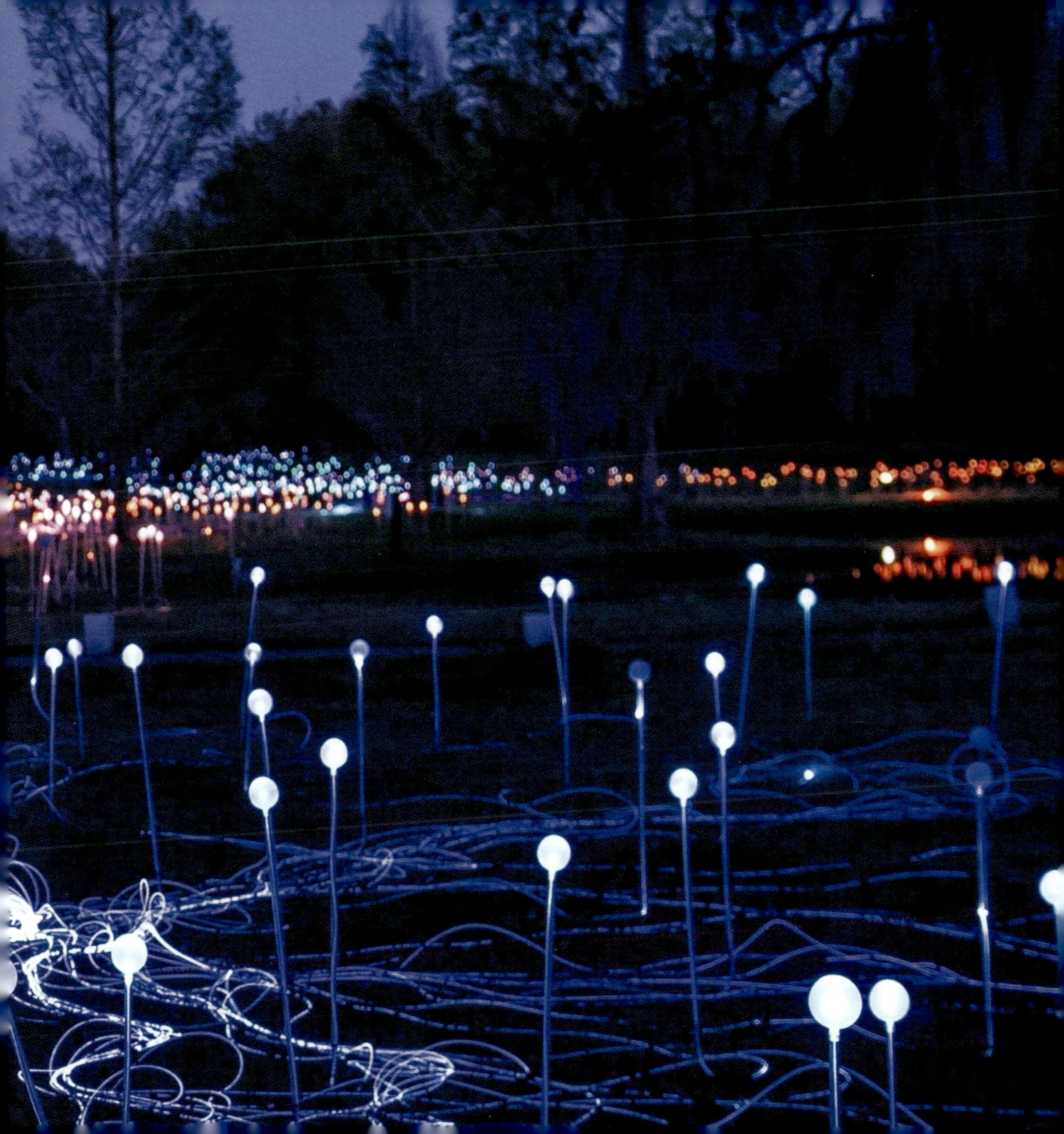

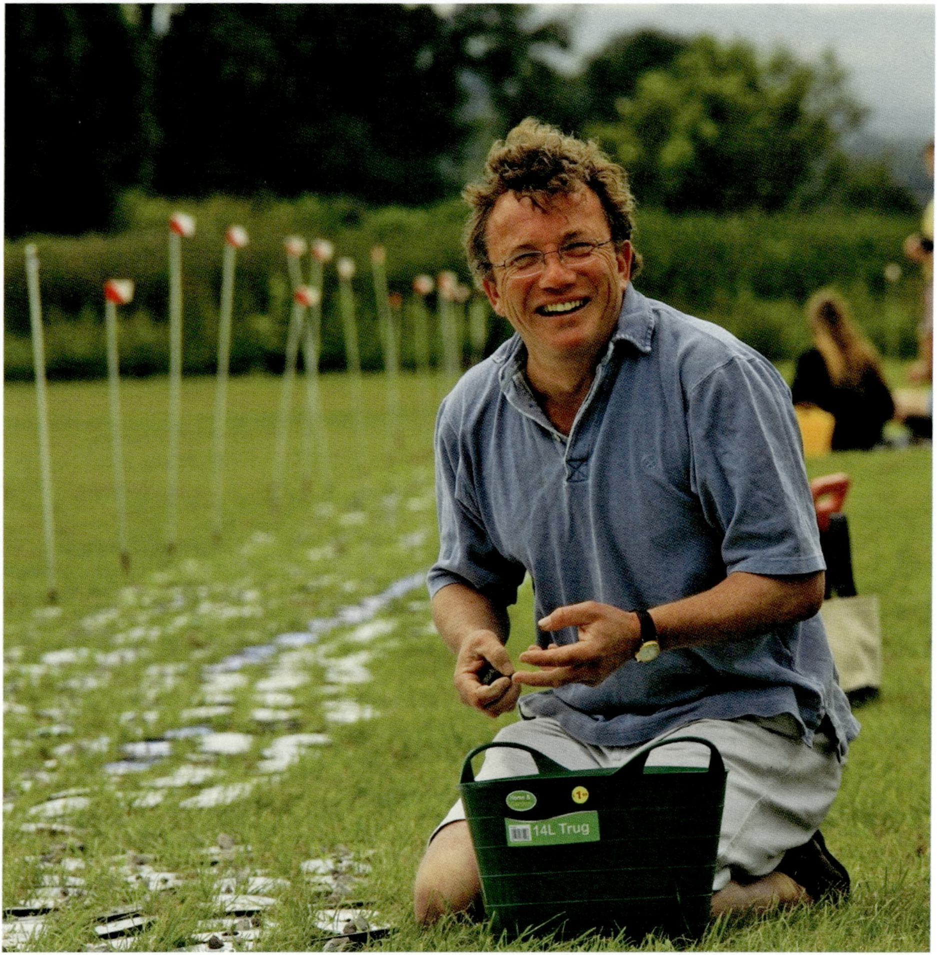

Bruce Munro, 2010.

CATCHING THE LIGHT

DR. RICHARD CORK

With spectacular audacity, Bruce Munro succeeded in transforming a large English field with 600,000 unwanted compact discs. Given by donors across the world, these discarded CDs were given new life by a team of volunteers walking over Long Knoll Field in Wiltshire. They included families with children, all of whom helped to lay out the discs so deftly that they ended up creating a vast blanket of silver. It emphasized the immensity encompassed by this ambitious work, which Munro called *CDSea*. And once it was complete, the entire shimmering installation was open to everyone who roamed along the public footpath bisecting Long Knoll Field. Rather than viewing it at a respectful and alienating distance, local people were able to experience *CDSea* in a very direct, visceral way. They must have felt like swimmers, poised on the edge of a glinting ocean. The ancient solidity of the field was replaced by a water-like alternative, and after its installation in June 2010, the summer sunshine often gave these discs an aura of intense optical vivacity.

In this respect, Munro was remaining true to the seminal experience that inspired *CDSea*. It happened in Australia, where he spent eight years after graduating from art school in Bristol. Munro made very little art during his Australian period, which commenced in 1984. But his subsequent work has benefited immeasurably from the stimulus provided by a few revelatory moments in the Antipodes. So far as *CDSea* was concerned, the epiphany occurred one Sunday afternoon when he escaped to Nielsen Park, a part of Sydney Harbour National Park, which provided

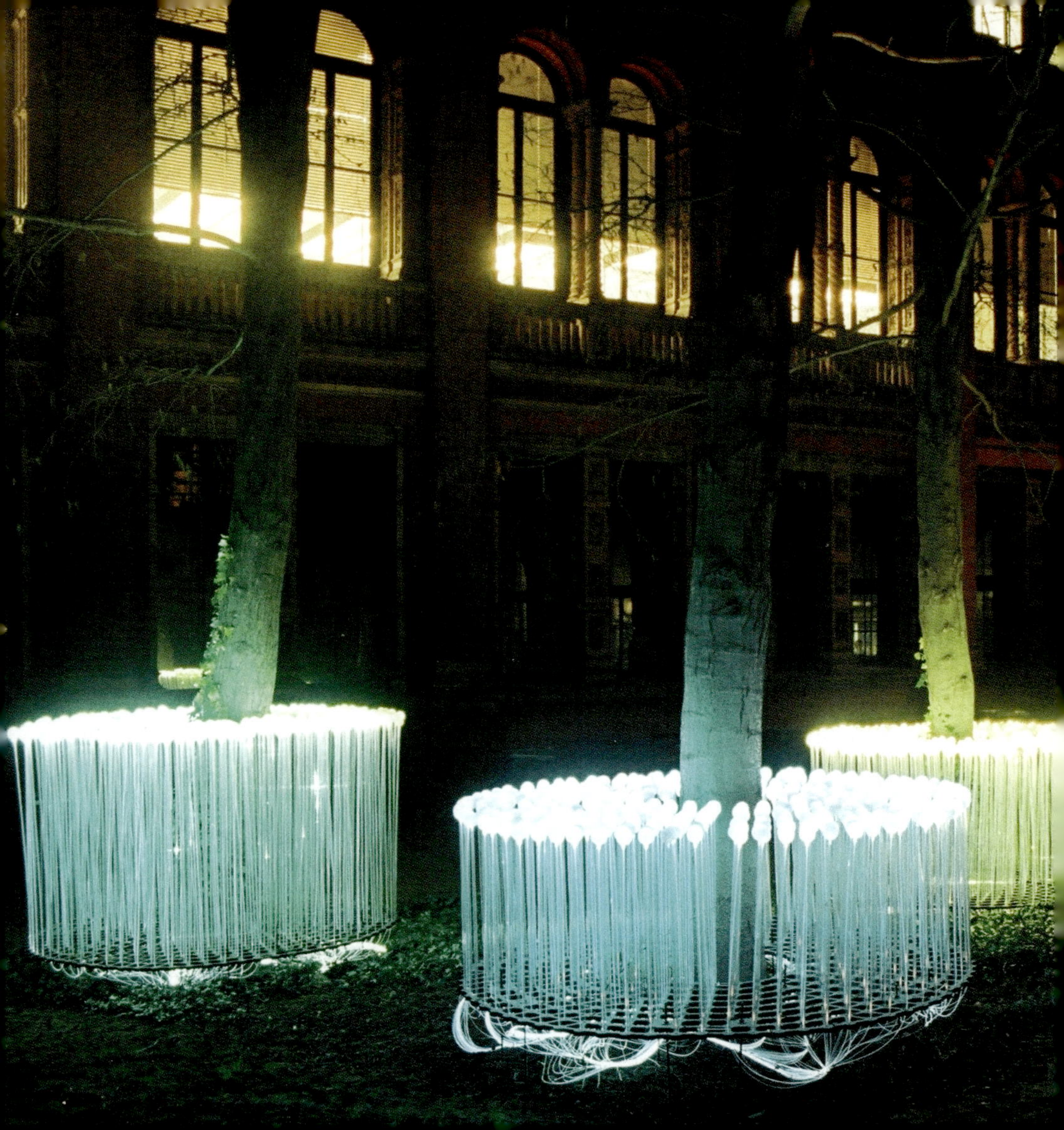

refuge from his weekday routine. Seated on a rocky peninsula, he gazed out to sea and found himself astonished by the sheer potency of the light. Munro's longing for England, and especially Salcombe in South Devon, where his father lived, was alleviated by the thought that the sun-saturated Sydney sea was linked, on a fundamental level, to the water lapping around Salcombe's coast. That is why Munro left Nielsen Park beach in a very positive mood, amazed that the play of light had changed his state of mind so profoundly. He now thinks that "it proved an unforgettable turning-point in my life."

Elsewhere, the irresistible power of Australian light would also nourish another of Munro's major sculptural installations. This time it happened in 1992 when he was journeying to Uluṟu through the barren red desert of central Australia. By a paradox, the extraordinary heat and brightness gave him a sustained energy. Every evening he would pull off the Stewart Highway and spend the night in a campsite. There, meditating quietly before sleep, Munro made on the pages of his ever-present sketchbook the first drawings for a work that has now undergone several fascinating permutations: *Field of Light*. As its title suggests, this installation comes alive at the onset of dusk. Suddenly, when the field grows dark and almost invisible, the stems of light that Munro planted there in thousands burst into bloom. He originally imagined them, during his epic 1992 expedition, flowering in the red desert as if nourished by a miraculous shower of rain.

During the first decade of the present century, when Munro's art reached maturity, *Field of Light* finally emerged in London. It made an arresting appearance in the *Brilliant!* exhibition at the Victoria & Albert Museum in summer 2004. And during the same year, a ten-acre version containing more than 15,000 individual stems of light was "planted" in Long Knoll Field. Through the seasons, he was able to scrutinize

Field of Light, *Victoria & Albert Museum, London, UK, 2004.*

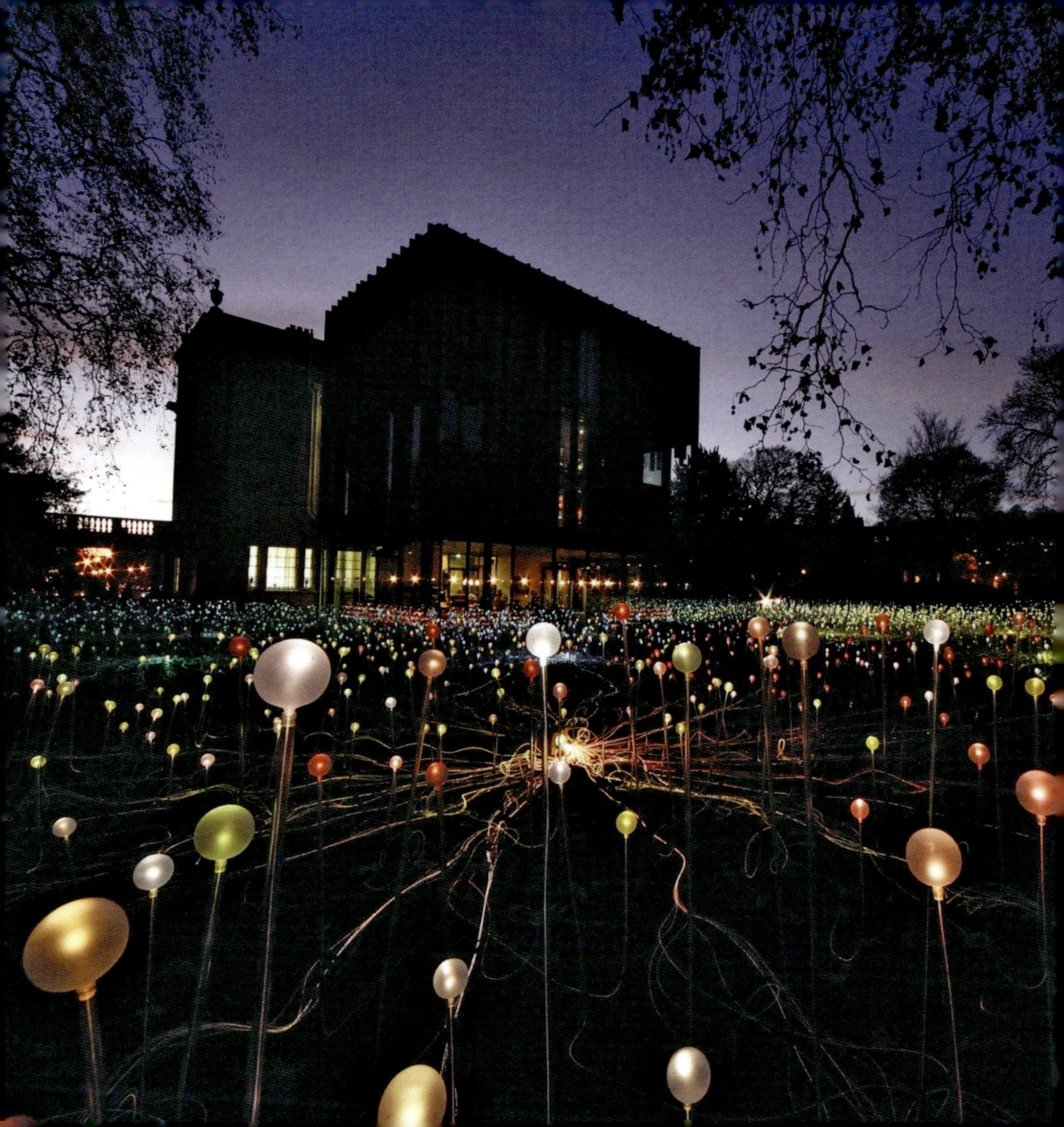

it from his nearby studio workshop until summer 2005, and thereafter Munro was given the opportunity to recreate *Field of Light* at the Eden Project in Cornwall. Here, between the Mediterranean and Rainforest "biomes," he installed 6,000 acrylic stems capped by frosted glass spheres. Laced with optic fiber, they were planted in the grass roof sheltering the visitors' center. All through the Cornish winter of 2008–09, *Field of Light* provided an affirmative and, at times, revelatory spectacle for people who encountered it. And in 2011, Munro installed a 5,200-stem *Field of Light* behind the Holburne Museum in Bath, where a major extension had just been designed with great success by the architect Eric Parry. In 2016, Munro installed *Field of Light*, with stems illuminated by custom-made solar power projectors, in the immense heartland at Uluṟu in central Australia

He has also been busy making pieces for landmark outdoor locations in the United States. Early in 2010 Munro was invited to create a solo exhibition for Longwood Gardens near Philadelphia, founded by Pierre S. du Pont. It opened two years later, and *Field of Light* played an important part in the show when it was spread across five acres of Longwood's Forest Walk to create *Forest of Light*. Subsequent exhibitions at Cheekwood Botanical Garden and Museum of Art in Nashville, Tennessee, and Franklin Park Conservatory and Botanical Gardens in Columbus, Ohio, were quickly proffered. At night, the garden visitors who discovered his sparkling assertion of multi-colored growth and luminosity had no difficulty understanding why Munro once declared that "light is my passion."

The origins of this central obsession can be traced back to a very early stage in his development. Munro's parents split up when he was six years old, and subsequently he always looked forward to visiting his father down on the coast at Salcombe. The exceptional allure of the natural surroundings enthralled him, and he still remembers

Field of Light, *Holburne Museum, Bath, UK, 2011.*

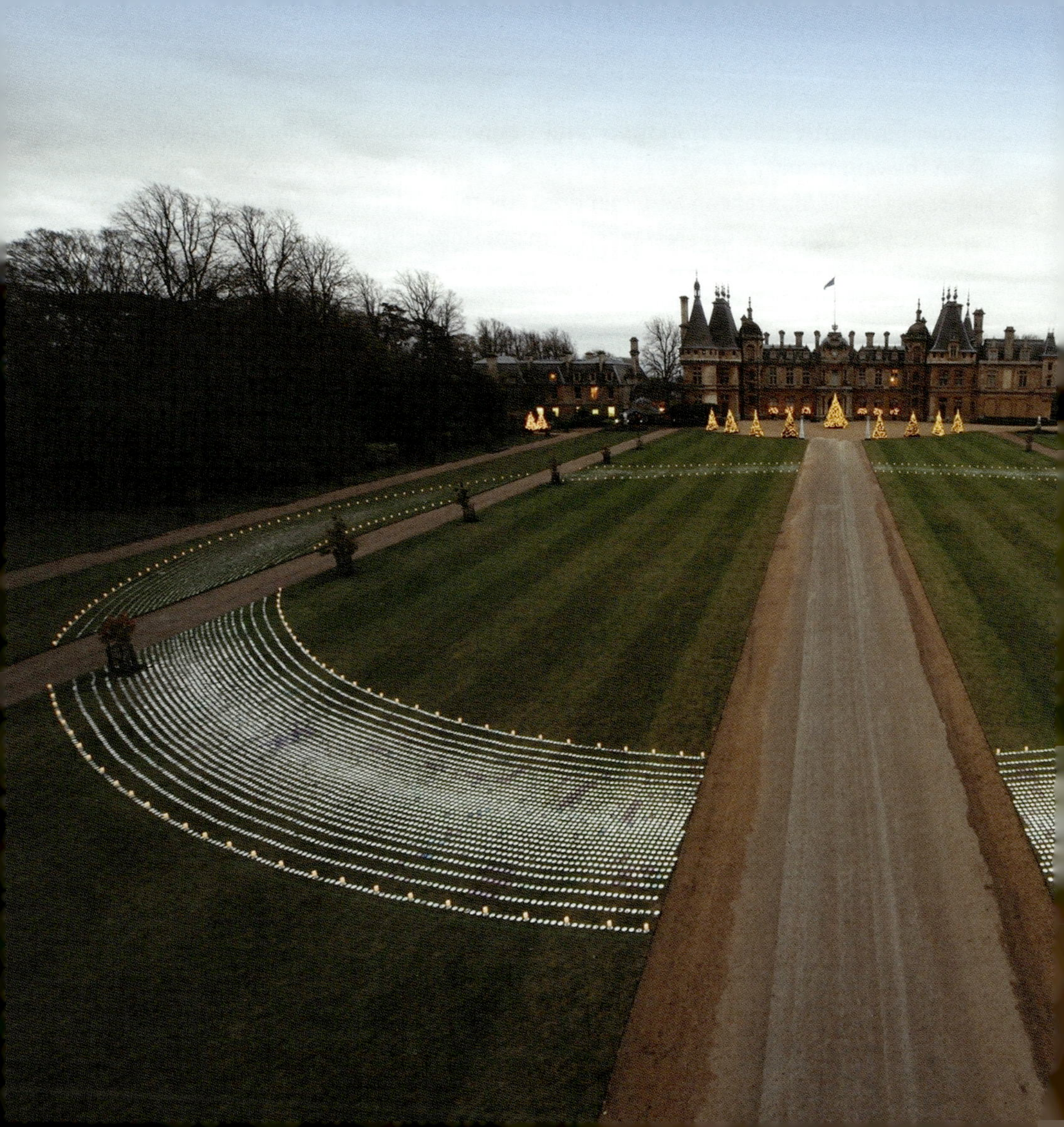

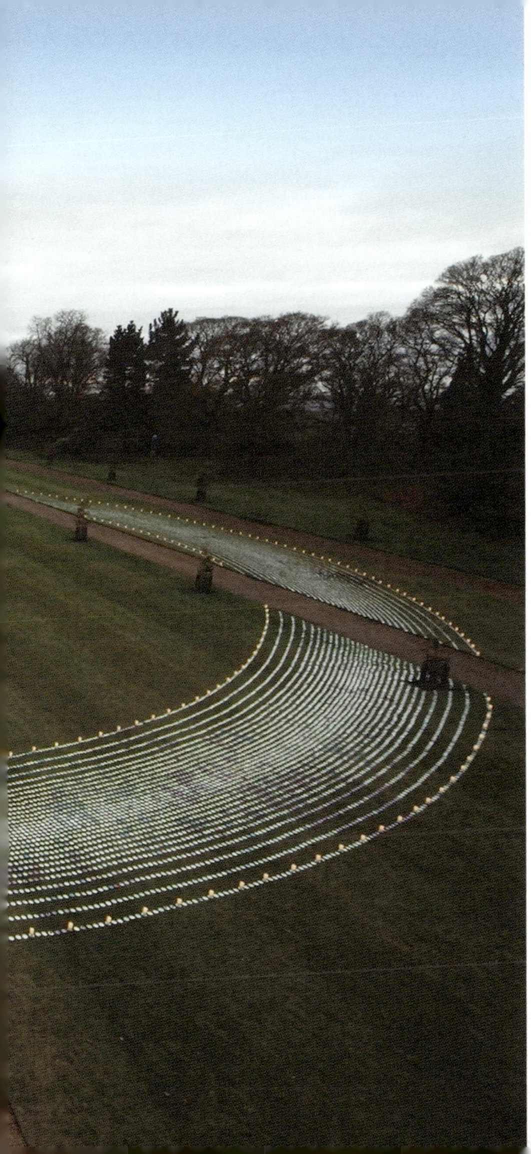

"when I was about eight walking from my father's house into Salcombe and thinking: 'When is the secret going to be revealed?' Because I thought there was an essence that was mysterious."

As a teenager, Munro got into trouble for his penchant for daydreaming, and he created his own private world in the pages of sketchbooks. Although they were often dismissed as mere escapism, the truth is that Munro's persistent dreams were all inspired by his alert, hungry response to the world around him. He recalls how "at the age of twenty-one, I was running down a path at home and smelling wild apricots on a beautiful autumn evening. Then I disappeared and felt as if I were floating across the ground. It was a magic moment, being at one with the world."

But he was not yet ready to give these visions a sculptural form. Munro had spent much of his adolescence

Angel of Light, *Waddesdon Manor, Buckinghamshire, UK, 2012.*

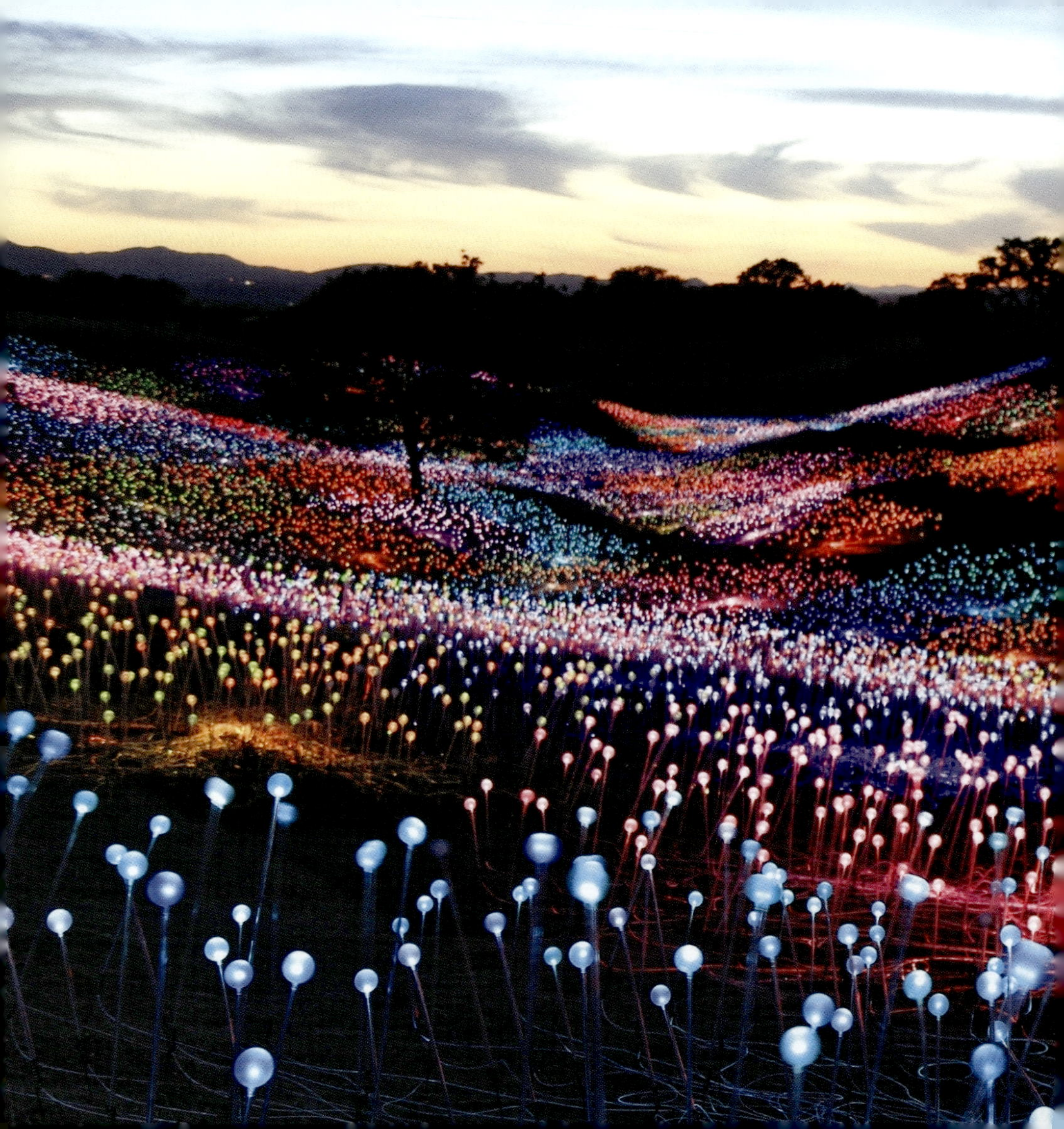

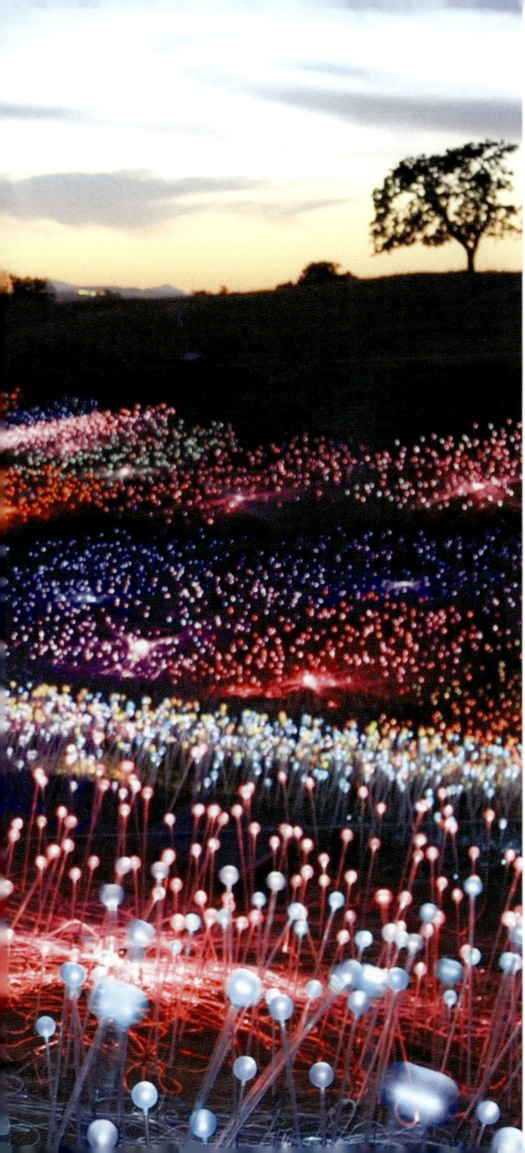

trying to paint his nightly dreams, and he was haunted by "images of a shark in a pool, big waves, and a mushroom cloud." Although he is now pursuing some of these nightmarish images, they led him nowhere during his teenage years. Even at art school Munro did not realize that sculpture was the prime area he should explore. Several painters commanded his particular respect as a student. He remembers admiring Matisse "because I felt he was so spiritual, and I adored Howard Hodgkin. I would love to make sculptures that have the feel of his paintings." Munro was also impressed by Georgia O'Keeffe's "beautifully haunting paintings," especially a large, late image of "clear blue sky populated by abstracted clouds that receded from the bottom to top edge of the canvas." Among the pioneering artists inspired by the land, he responded to James Turrell as well as Richard Long, who had started out studying

Field of Light, *Sensorio, Paso Robles, California, USA, 2019.*

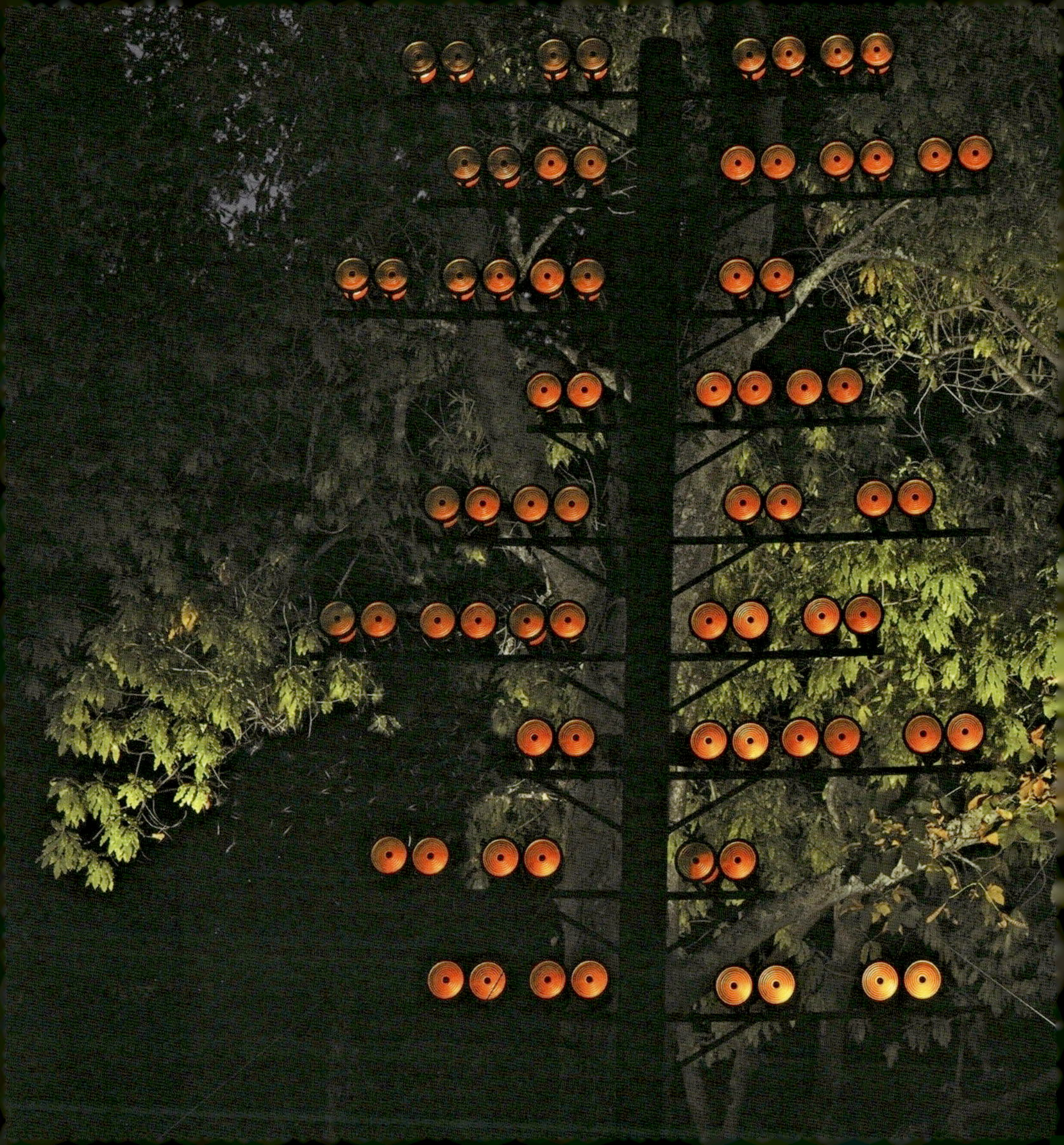

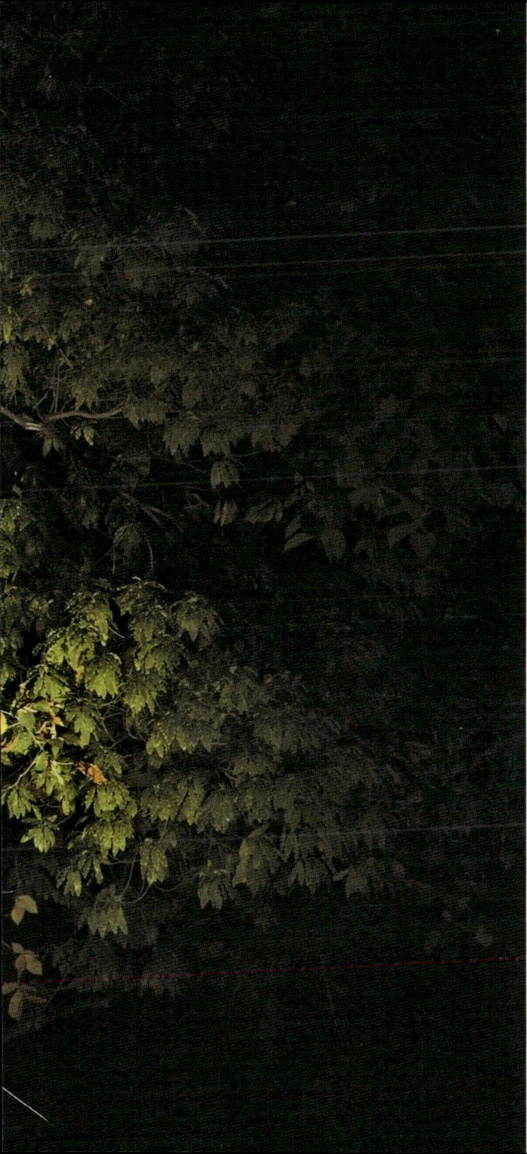

at the same art school in Bristol. And Munro has never forgotten watching a mesmeric film of a road, *Last Chants for a Slow Dance*, by the independent American filmmaker Jon Jost.

Book-reading likewise played a significant part in nourishing Munro's emergent imagination. Although he was "a late and slow reader, and never found it easy," his cousin brought books by C.S. Lewis to the family house. Munro's boyhood memories of the Chronicles of Narnia were still alive enough in his mind to trigger a work called *Parliament of Owls*. His first thoughts for this piece were stimulated by a glass lens that reminded Munro of a caricatured owl's eye. But then he recalled that in *The Silver Chair*, of The Chronicles of Narnia, a collection of owls was called a "parliament." Hence his decision to mount a whole collection of glass eyes on a telegraph pole that he had removed from the Long Knoll Field before

Parliament of Owls, *Montalvo Arts Center, Saratoga, California, USA, 2018.*

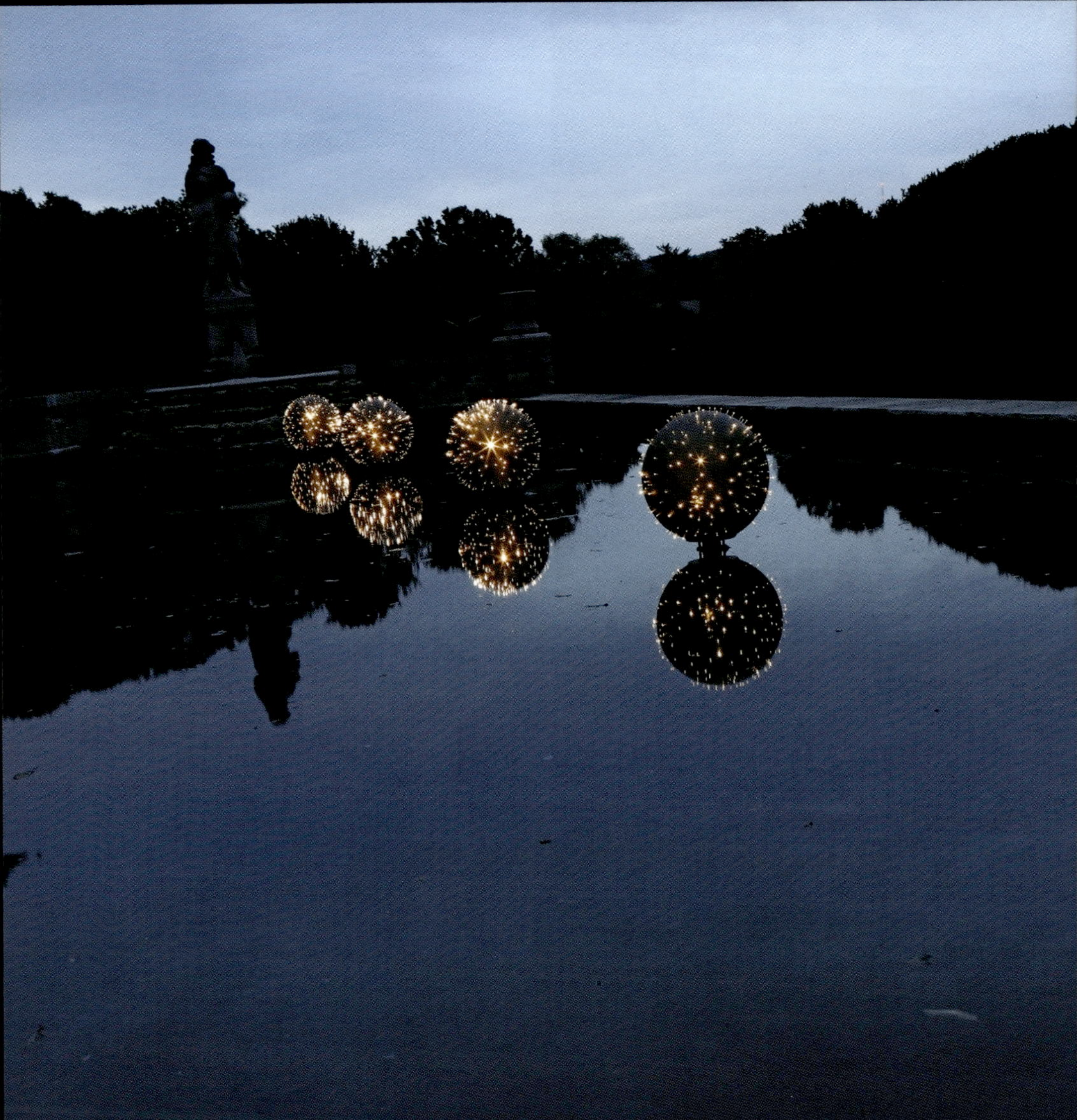

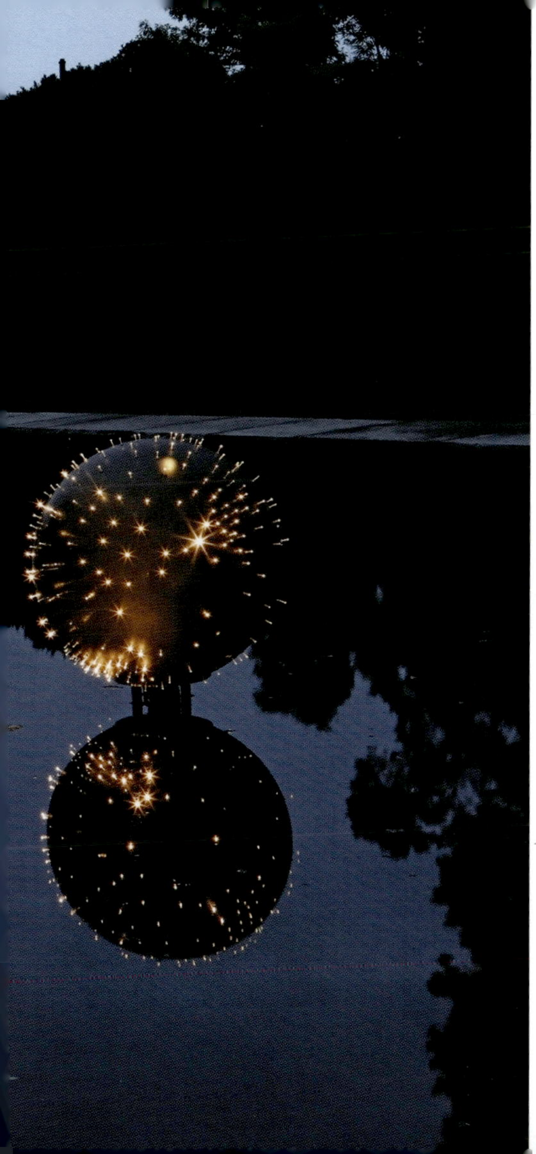

burying the power lines underground. Munro always relishes finding new uses for discarded materials, and the telegraph pole was triumphantly restored to an upright position for its new role in *Parliament of Owls*, finally to be executed at Waddesdon Manor in 2013.

Another important source of literary inspiration was Lyall Watson's book *Gifts of Unknown Things*. Munro read this radical text when he was twenty-one, and became captivated by the young girl Tia who lives on an island in the Indonesian archipelago. Very mysteriously, she can respond to sounds by seeing them in color. And Tia's magical ability gave Munro the crucial starting-point for an elaborate, maze-like work called *Water-Towers*. In 2011, this dramatically illuminated sequence of 69 monumental structures, each containing 252 recyclable water bottles, was installed in the

Fagin's Urchins, *Cheekwood Botanical Garden and Museum of Art, Tennessee, USA, 2013.*

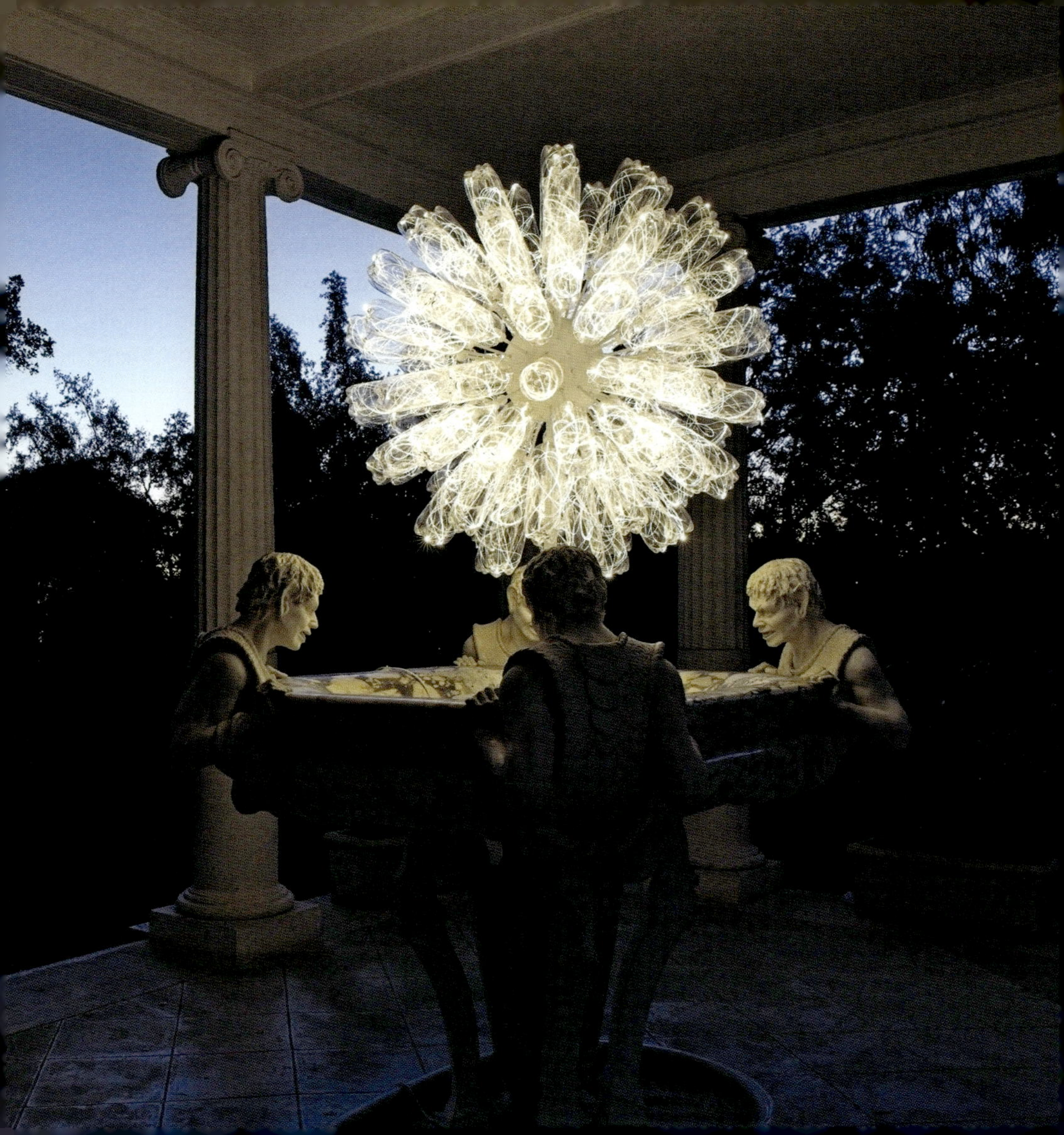

Cloisters at Salisbury Cathedral, one of the most aspirant Gothic buildings in Britain. Munro stacked the bottles and lit them with optic fibers, which responded to the sound of choral music. Visitors were invited to make their way through this dazzling maze and found themselves caught up in the synchronized rainbow of colors. They irradiated the people as well as the architecture, while inside the Cathedral a breathtaking *Light Shower* installation cascaded from the Spire Crossing. Munro succeeded in transforming the place where the transepts intersect with the nave, sending no less than 2,000 optic fibers floating downwards before they terminated in clear diffusers shaped like teardrops. The piece was illuminated to herald the beginning of Advent, when a candle-lit procession moved through the Cathedral celebrating the significance of the Advent Procession "From Darkness to Light."

By no means are all of Munro's recent works as affirmative in mood. Like everyone, he has been affected by the pessimism and fear plaguing a Western world still shaken by military aggression and, above all, economic gloom. In his vision for *Last Charge*, he brings together 600 wooden clothes horses with 3,365 fencers and 6,730 discarded fluorescent tubes to create an outdoor area of stroboscopic light. Its flashing urgency evokes the appalling tragedy of the Light Brigade's futile charge in the battle of Balaclava. Lord Cardigan led this doomed cavalry assault during the Crimean War of 1854, and Munro's soundtrack of thundering hooves encourages everyone to visualize the riders hurtling to their tragic destination. Seen in its entirety, *Last Charge* looks like a flickering graveyard of fallen hopes.

An even more ominous project is *The Last Wave*, a traumatic image that can be traced back to Peter Weir's film of the same name. Munro saw it on BBC television in 1984, just before he left his native country and moved to Australia. Eight years later, while making a farewell trip around Australia with his fiancée, Serena, Munro

Bacchus' Spring, *Montalvo Arts Center, Saratoga, California, USA, 2018.*

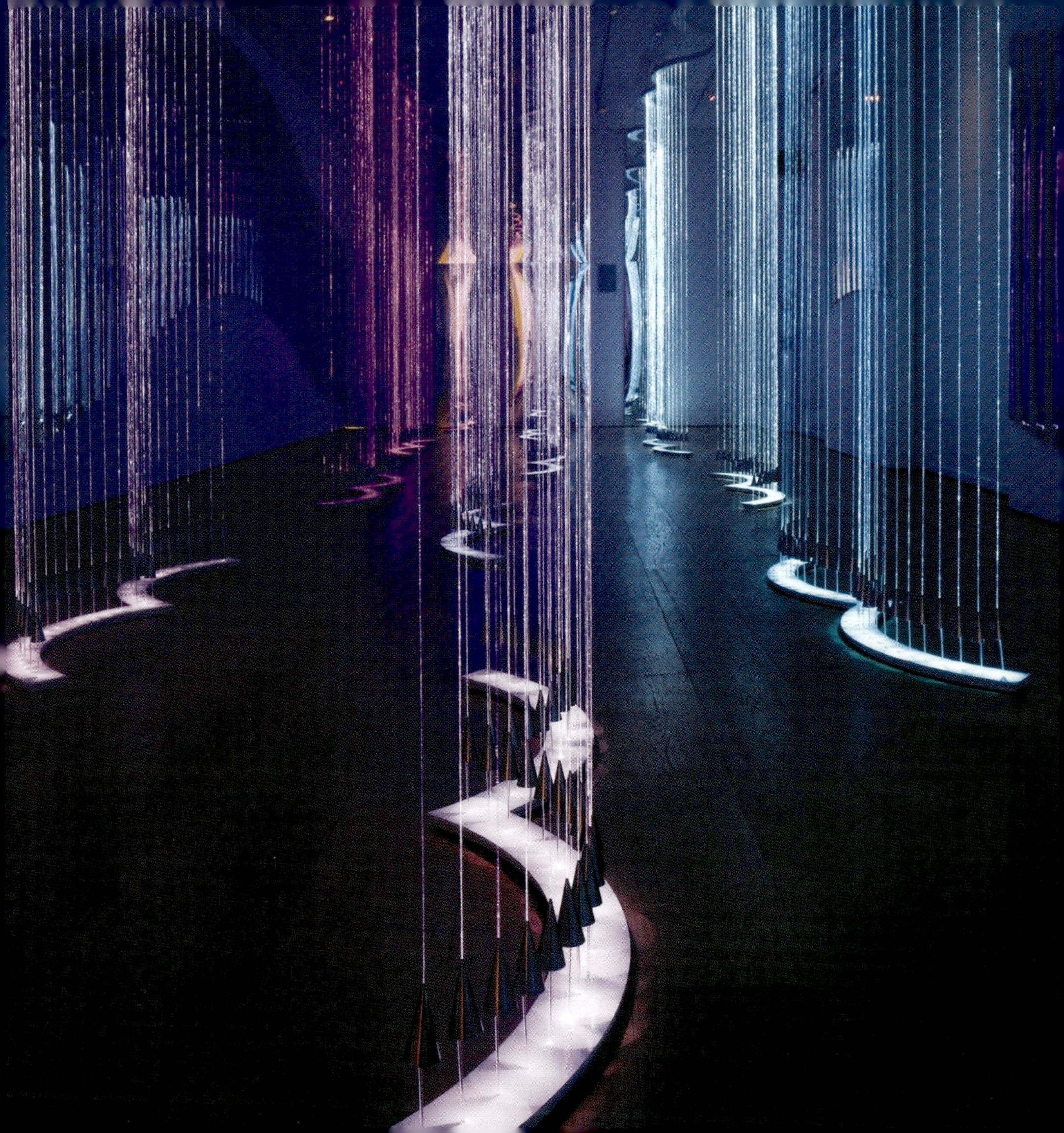

was still so haunted by memories of the film that he dreamed about a tsunami-like wall of water curving high over Sydney. He determined to recreate its impact, using 2.5 million black mussel-shell casts suspended in mid-air and glowing with fiber-optic cables. This looming apparition would clearly be an unnerving spectacle, and sum up the apocalyptic anxieties that often invade twenty-first-century consciousness today.

Ultimately, however, Munro is sustained by an obstinate and fundamental spirit of optimism. At Waddesdon Manor, the magnificent property built in Buckinghamshire by Baron Ferdinand de Rothschild, Munro has made an evocative installation in 2013 called *Cantus Arcticus*. Music once again played a major role in bringing this work to the forefront of Munro's imagination. He heard on the radio a symphony with this title by the Finnish composer Einohujani Rautavaara. Its sublime soundscape captivated him, and after downloading a copy of the music, he listened to it time and again. Such obsessive concentration led Munro to create, for the capacious interior of Waddesdon's Coach House at the Stables, an evocation of the Northern Lights and the frozen landscape of the Arctic tundra. Abstracted forms inspired by seabirds can be found here, suspended in a space where curtains of fiber-optic strands are fortified by steel cone bells. Veils of light cascading from above create an all-pervasive luminosity and cast soft pools of color that alter in response to the unfolding drama of Rautavaara's symphony. *Cantus Arcticus* testifies to the enduring power of music in Munro's current work, but he also regards the Waddesdon installation as an act of homage to Kama, the Hindu god of love. Munro is convinced that Rautavaara's music is "a holistic interpretation of the beauty and wonder of life itself, in this instance the lives of humans and birds."

After the death of Munro's father in 1999, Munro suffered a crisis and then benefited

Cantus Arcticus, *Waddesdon Manor, Buckinghamshire, UK, 2013.*

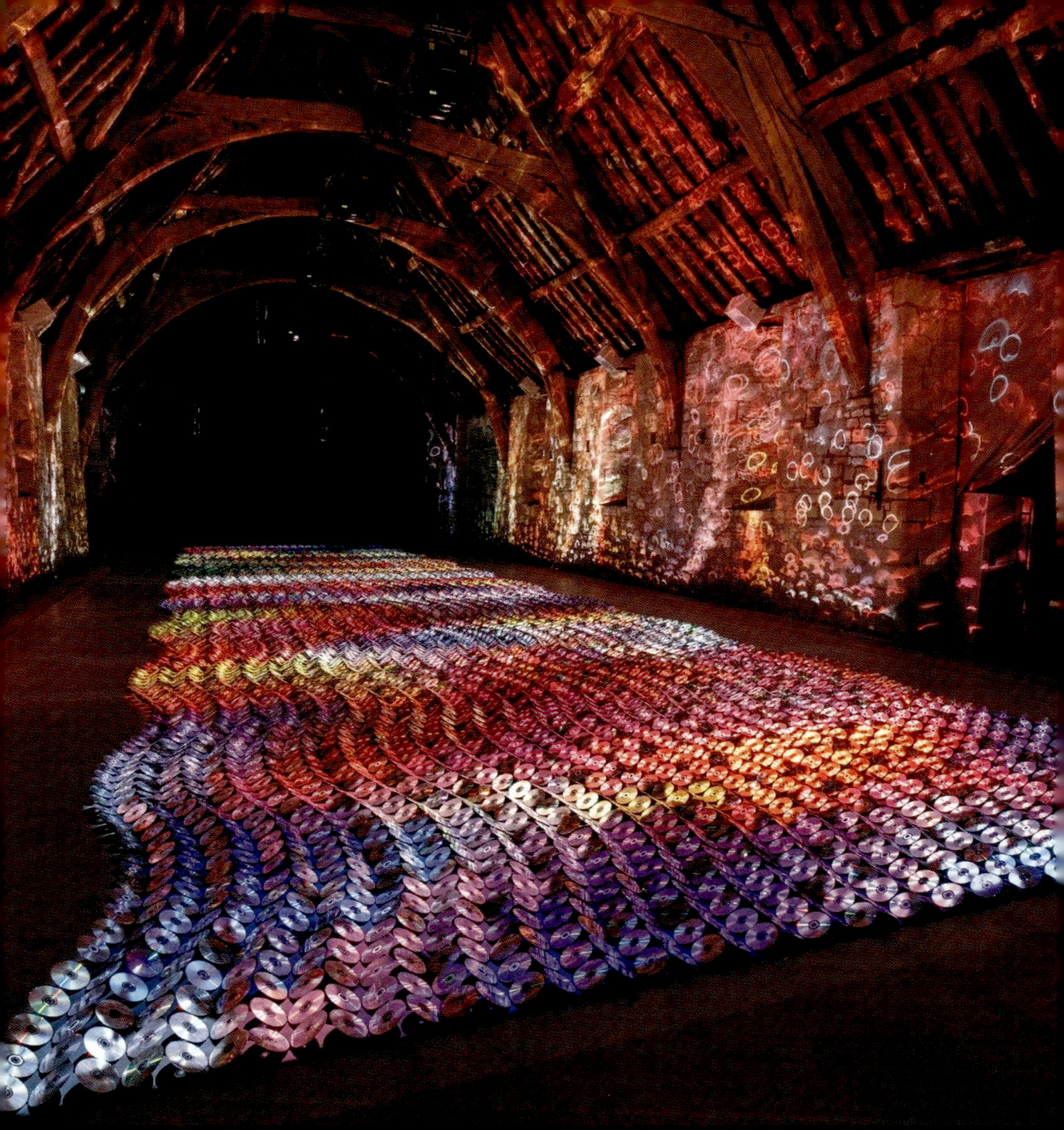

from the healing power of meditation. It enabled him to realize the importance of focusing above all on being at one with the world, and this sense of unity finally helped him to develop his mature vision as an artist. Although most of his outdoor works are temporary, one of his most ambitious projects centers on the creation of a building called *Mettabhavana*. It originated in a Barbados beachside house, where he was staying with his family in 1997. On the first night, Munro dreamed that he saw a mysterious building from which light softly emanated, generating an aura of peacefulness. He completed the design of just such an elemental structure, reassuring in mood and accompanied on all sides by water in elliptical pools—during the day illuminated by the sun, and at night by beeswax candles. He sees it essentially as a place where Metta Bhavana, the loving-kindness meditation, can be practiced by everyone who enters its calm, luminous interior.

While riding his bicycle in 2009, Munro remembered the undulating pathway in *CDSea* and realized that it linked up with the spiritual river that appears in two of the books he most admires. In *Kim*, Rudyard Kipling describes an arrow passing "far beyond sight" before falling and creating a river of limitless beneficence. In the other book, *Siddhartha* by Herman Hesse, "The river looked at him with a thousand eyes: green ones, white ones, crystal ones, sky-blue ones." It sounds uncannily like a description of Munro's glinting installations, and when Siddhartha "listened attentively to the thousandfold song of the river . . . to all of them, the whole, when he perceived the unity," then at last he "ceased to struggle with fate, ceased to suffer. On his face bloomed the cheerfulness of wisdom that is no longer opposed by will, that knows perfection, that is in harmony with the river of what is, with the current of life." Of all the connections across music, science, and literature that feed Munro's multi-faceted art, these heartfelt words sum up the essence of his vision with disarming eloquence.

C-Scales, *Messums Wiltshire, Wiltshire, UK, 2020.*
Over: Field of Light, *Uluṟu, at Voyages Ayers Rock Resort, Northern Territories, Australia, 2015.*

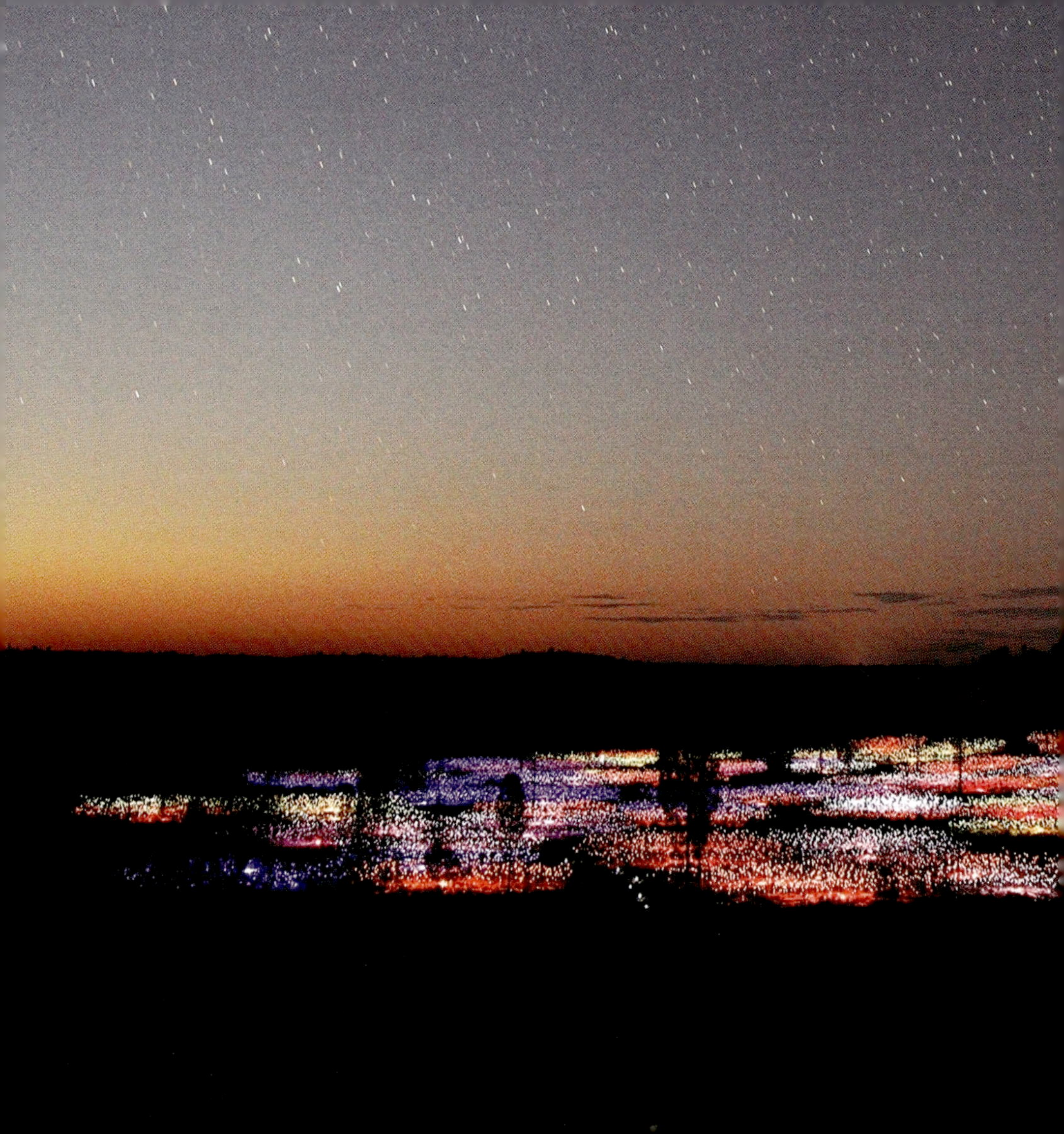

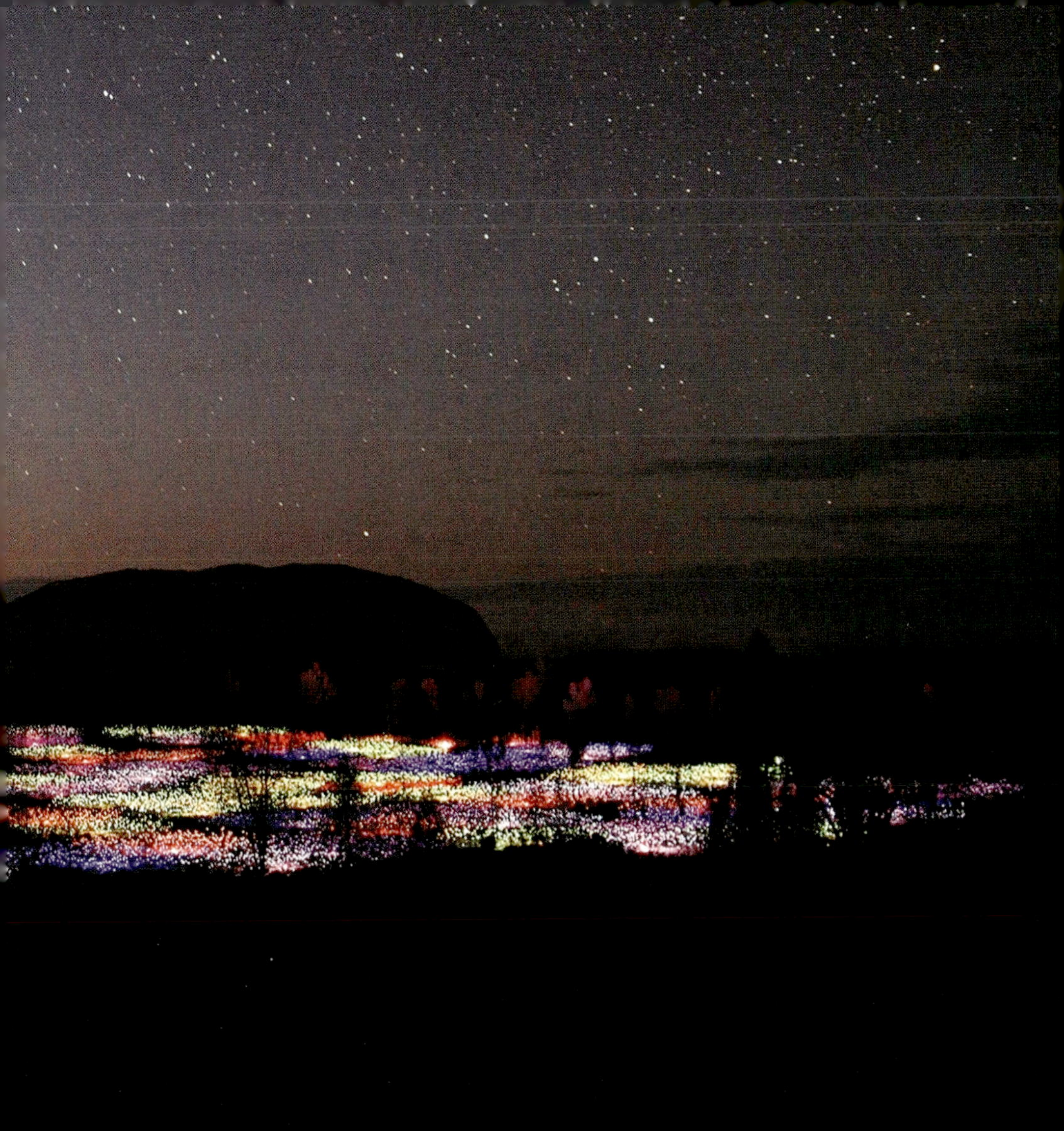

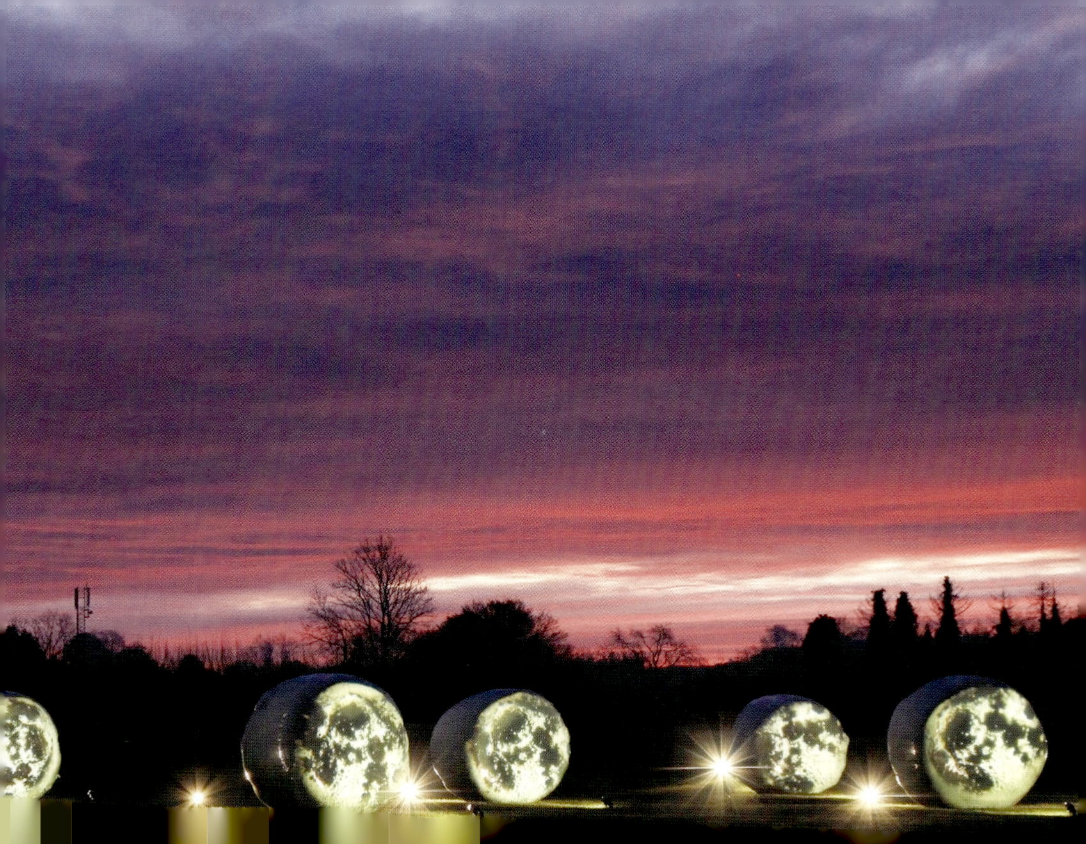

INSPIRATIONS

BRUCE MUNRO

I discovered light as a medium first in my professional career, outside of fine art. I had studied painting during my school and degree education in Britain, but I needed to earn a living and found myself doing that in Australia, manufacturing display signs using a glowing ultraviolet plastic whose properties I loved. When I decided to work in light, I chose it very carefully because I knew I needed some kind of focus. I thought that working in a medium that was very pure and true would simplify my ability to express all the different ideas that filled my head.

At first, the light things I was making were really lighting design. Then in my early forties, I began making things that were personal. I realized that I had always been striving to be so different—to make my art different—but starting then, I began looking for shared experience. Our experiences of being connected to the world in its largest sense, of being part of an essential pattern, became my subject matter.

Of the artworks I've had the privilege to make so far, *Field of Light, CDSea,* and *Water-Towers* have come most purely from moments of crystallized consciousness, memories of feelings that stood out so strongly that, years later, I could clearly put my finger on that emotional spot. Other pieces, like *Light Shower,* are a response to a particular space, and the opportunity to develop a component that will create the effect that I want. More and more, as I am offered the opportunity to consider specific sites, those two urges connect, and the artwork becomes about both the memory and the space. I have so many more pieces I can't wait to make.

Moon Harvest, *Messums Wiltshire, Wiltshire, UK, 2020.*

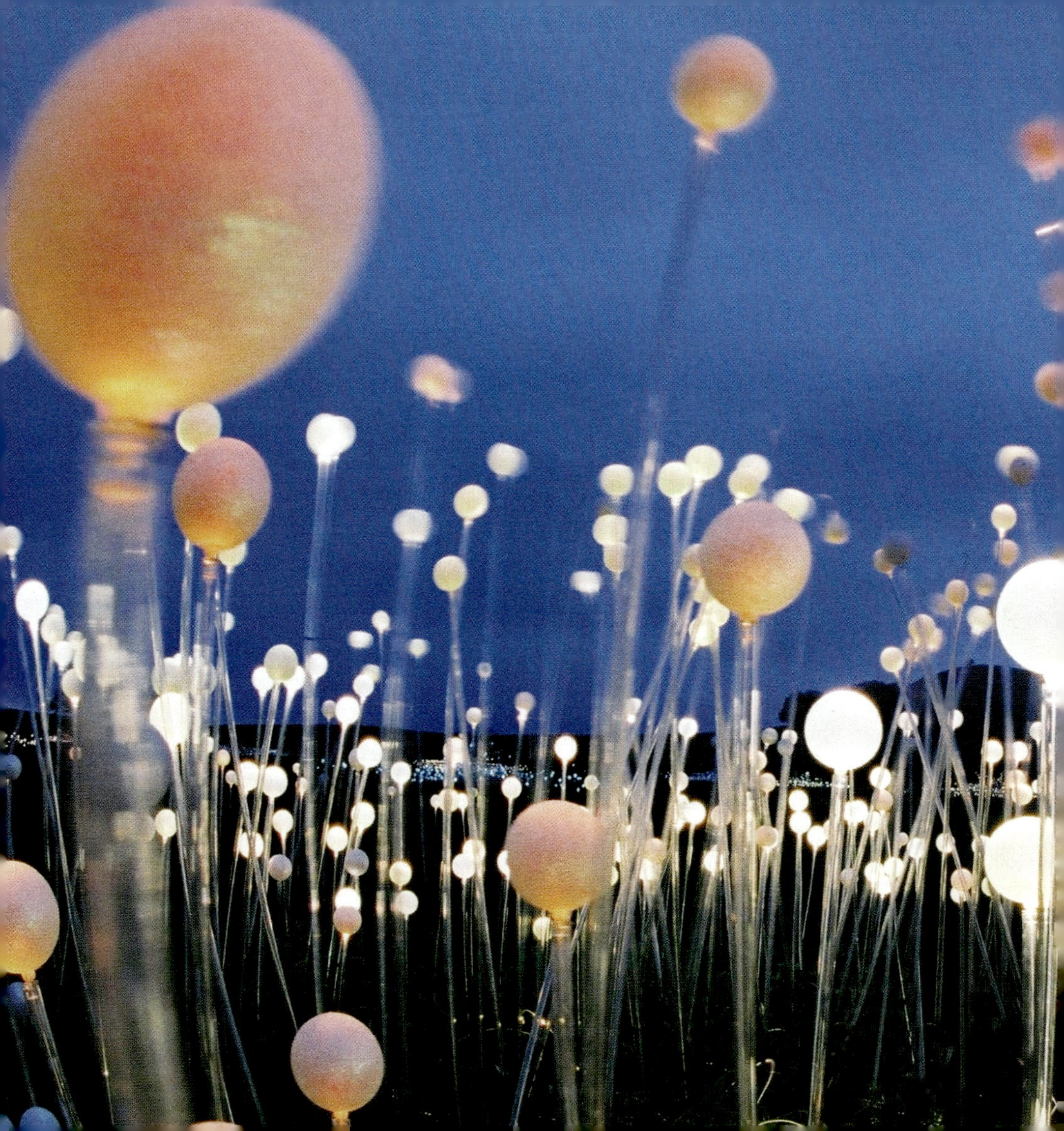

FIELD OF LIGHT

The *Field of Light* was originally conceived in 1992 during a trip through central Australia. The red desert had an incredible feeling of energy; ideas radiated from it along with the heat. The *Field of Light* installation was one idea that landed in my sketchbook and kept on nagging at me to be done.

The very first *Field of Light* was sown under the shadow of an ancient hill behind my home in southwest England in 2004. By placing an alien installation in the midst of nature, the enormous contrast created allows one to literally see the wood from the trees. One's attention is thus drawn to the nature that surrounds the installation as well as to the *Field of Light* itself. This contrast has always been an important focus since the idea germinated.

Laid out across a field of clover bisected by a public footpath, the first *Field of Light* shimmered its way through the seasons, presenting a myriad of opportunities for passersby to catch glimpses of the piece interacting with nature in all her guises. I am hopeful that every iteration of the *Field of Light* will inspire both young and old to take from it and create something of their own to pass on to others.

In recent years, I have had many more ideas about the meaning of the *Field of Light* and an equal number of ways to express these thoughts, but my instinct tells me that is not what I am meant to do, other than say the *Field of Light* is a personal symbol for the good things in life. My job is to make it happen and inspire those around me to join the project. I hope that it will gather its own momentum, and like the proverbial snowball, take on a life of its own when it reaches critical mass.

Field of Light, *Long Knoll, Wiltshire, UK, 2004.*
Over: Field of Light, *Franklin Park Conservatory and Botanical Gardens, Ohio, USA, 2013.*
Field of Light, *Avenue of Honour, Albany, Australia, 2018.*
Moon Bloom, *Messums Wiltshire, Wiltshire, UK, 2020.*

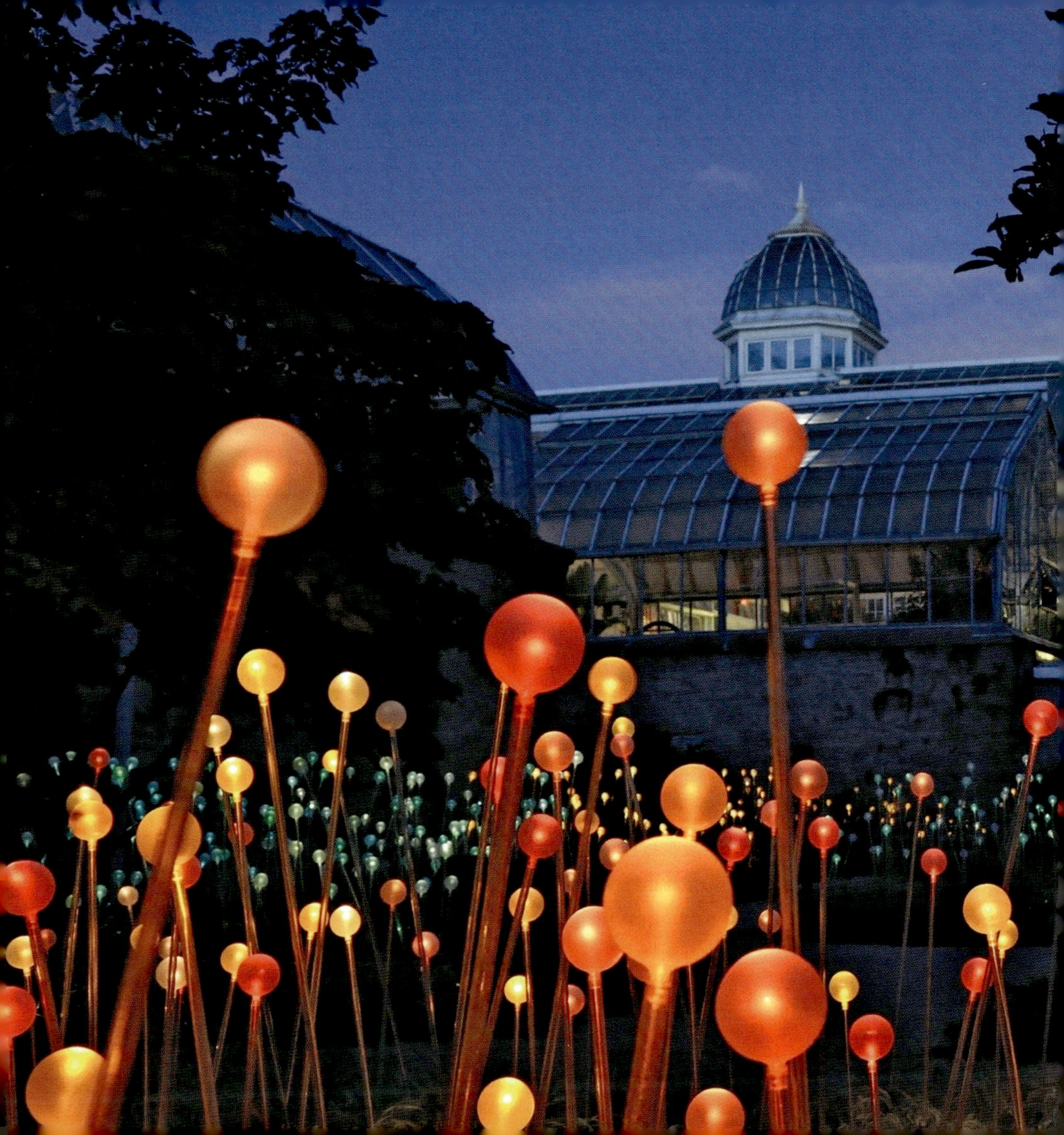

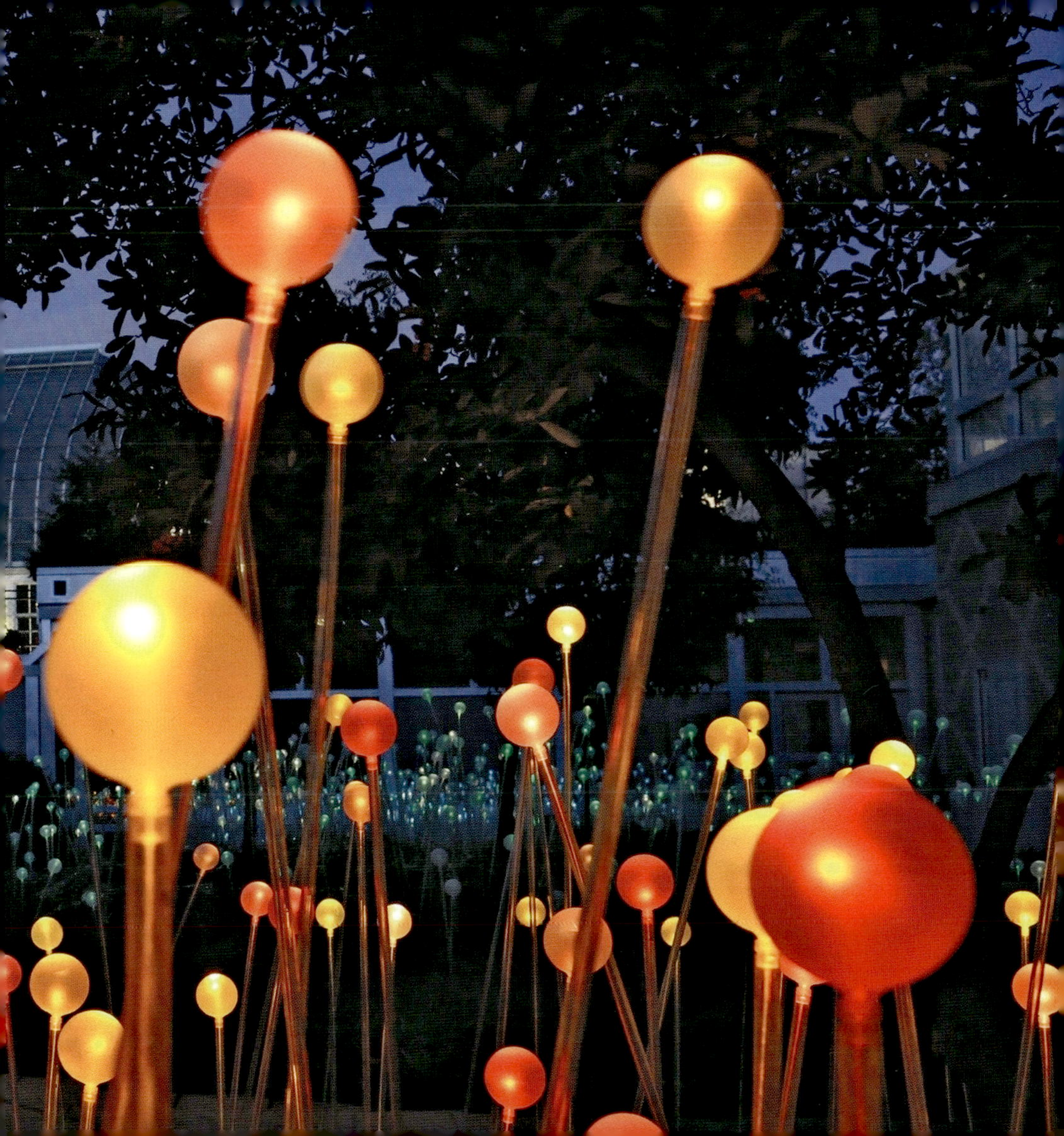

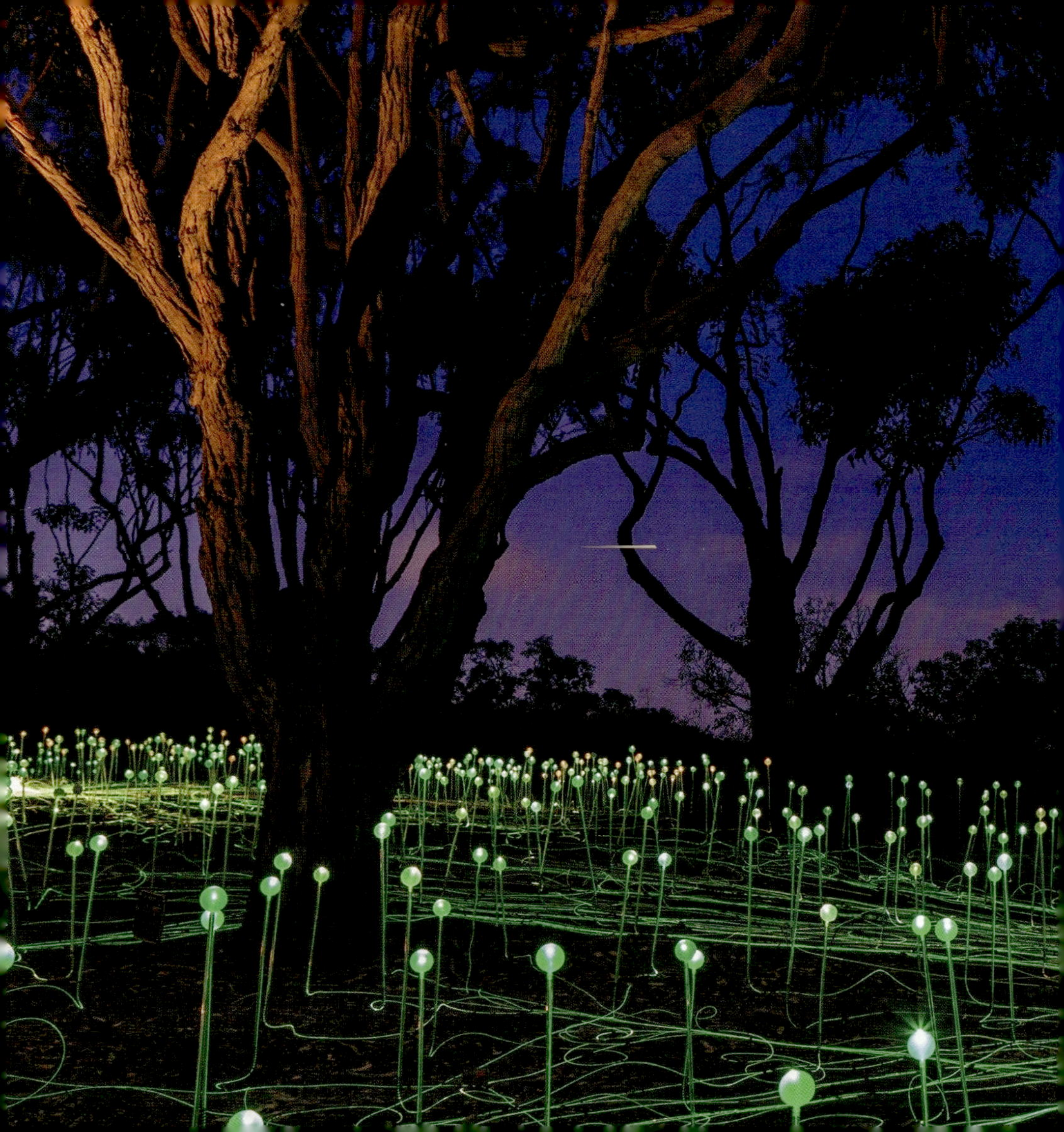

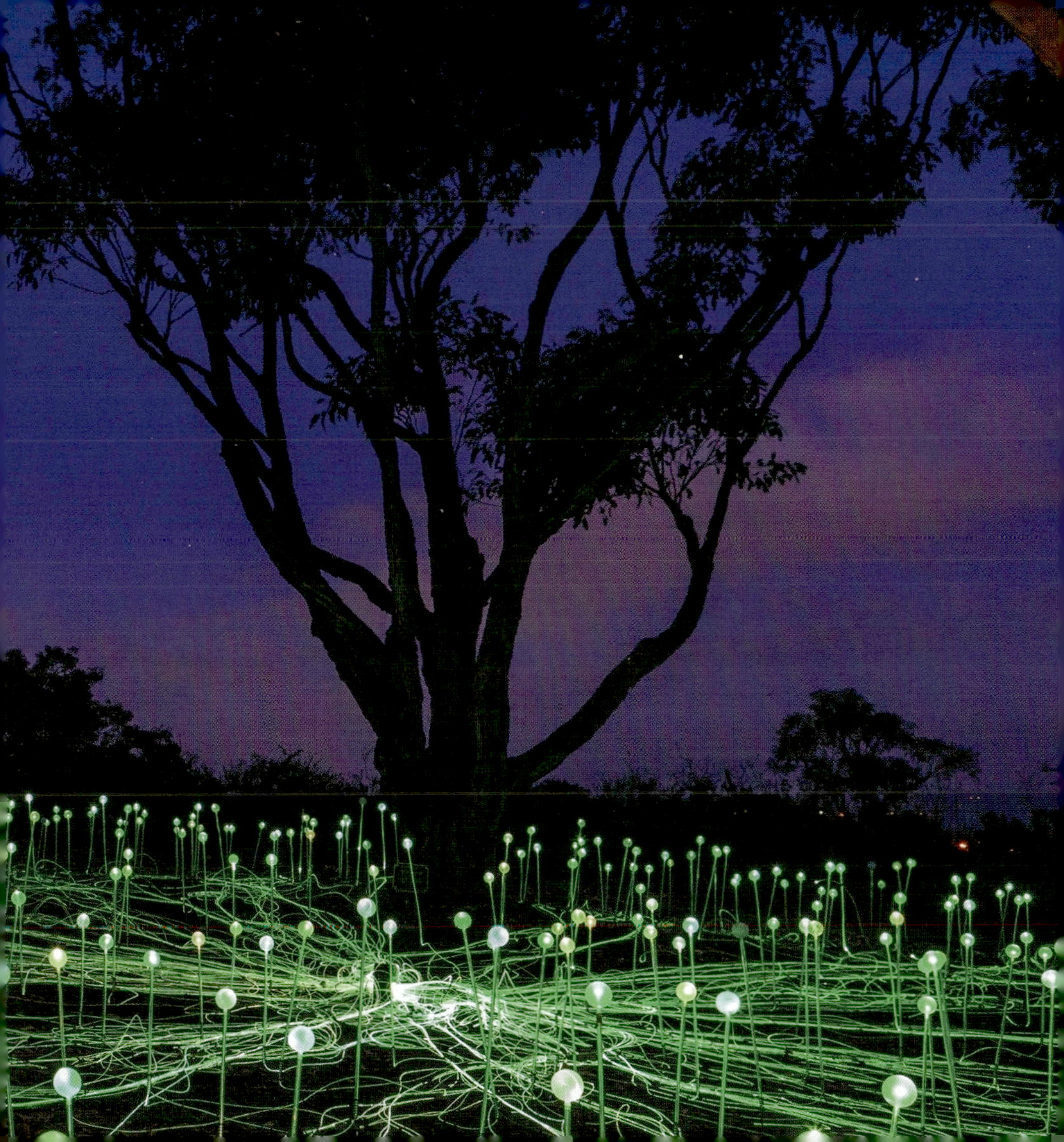

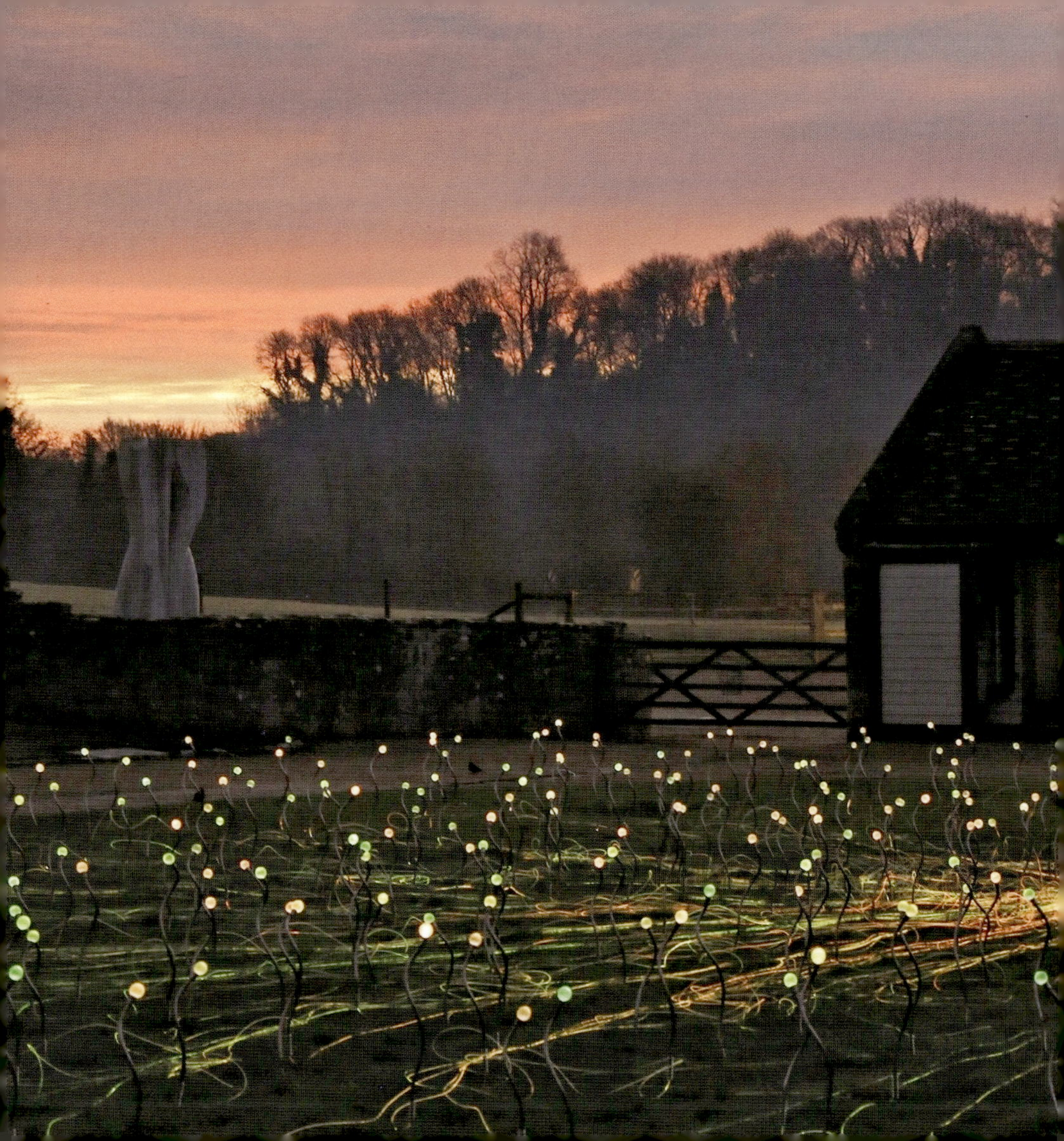

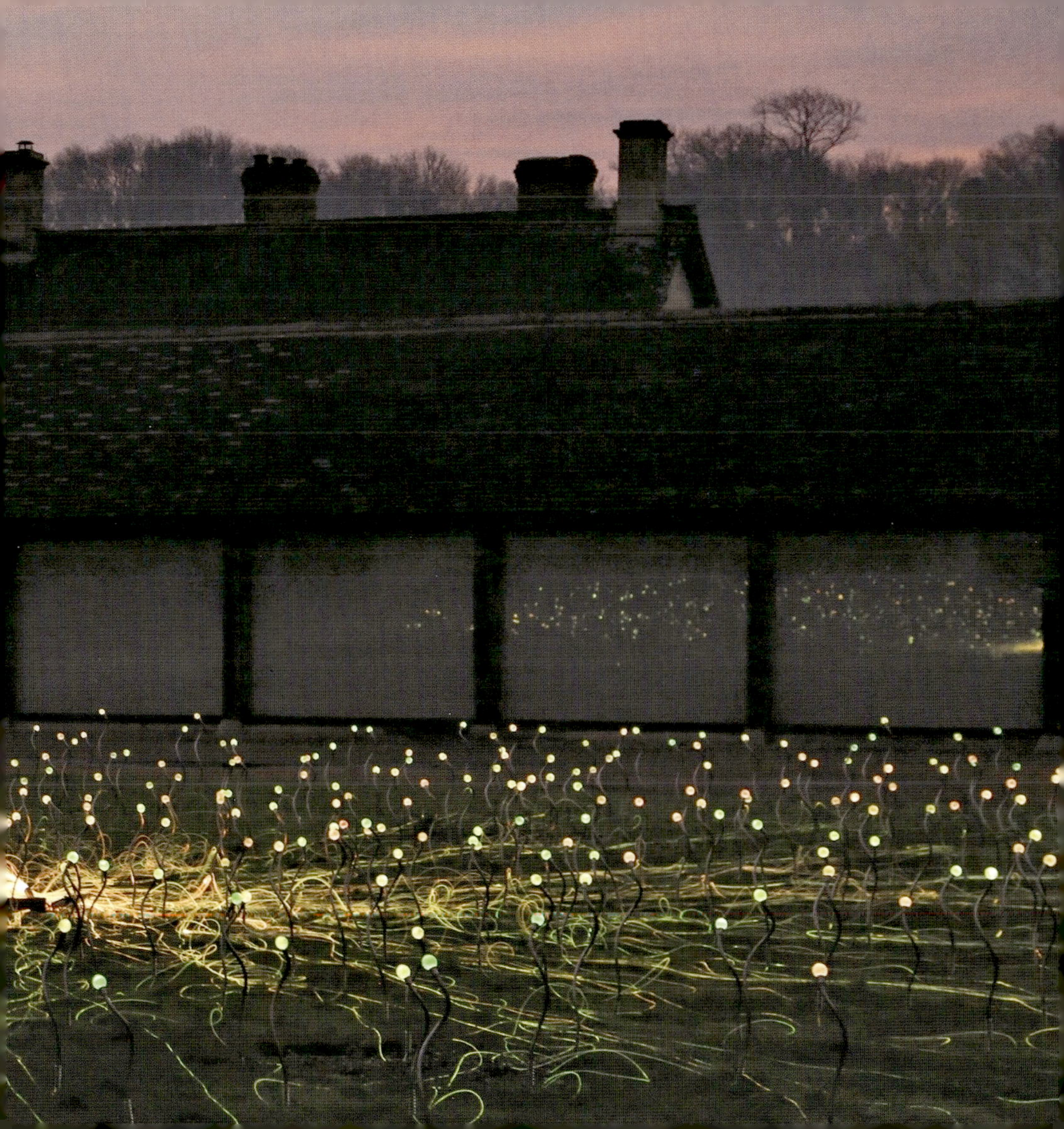

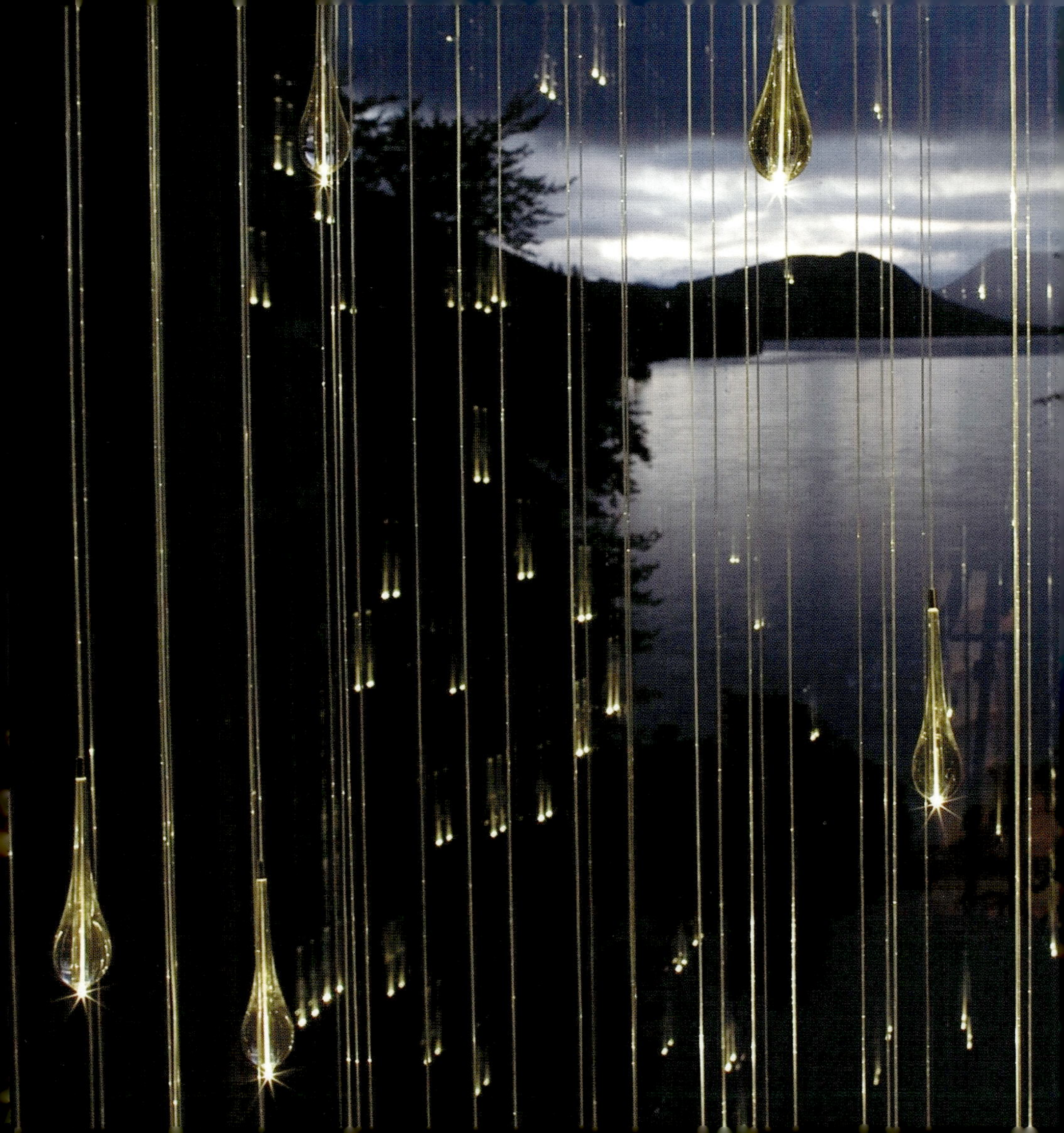

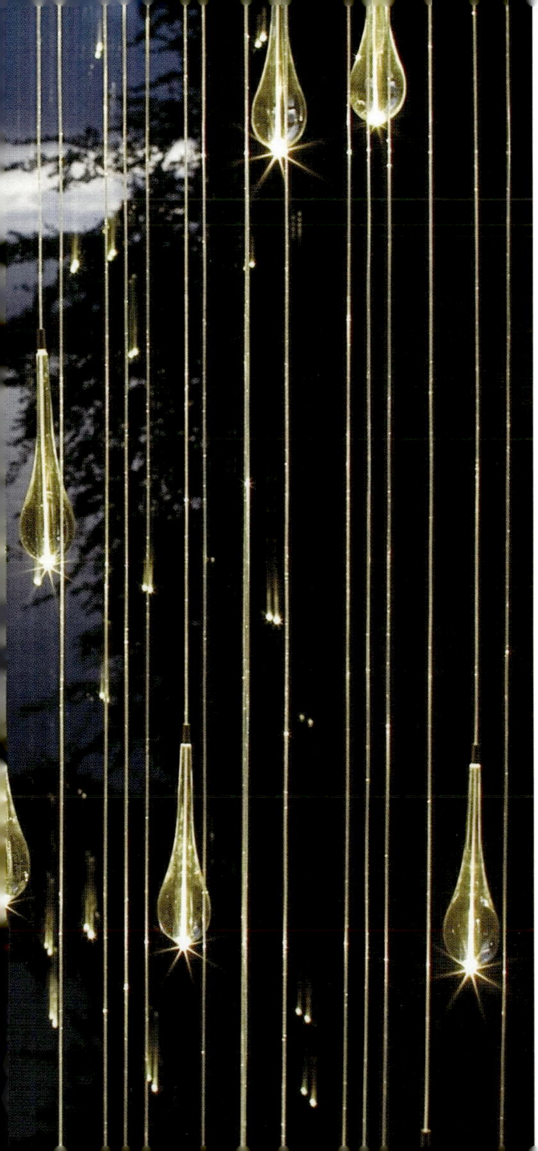

LIGHT SHOWER

In 2008, I was working on a design for a Highland lodge in Loch Ossian in Scotland. I found myself sitting on a step halfway up the main stairs of the lodge absorbing a magnificent, uninterrupted view of the loch and group of snow-capped mountains beyond. It was raining in squalls against the plate-glass window, which distorted the view with rivulets of water streaming down the panoramic pane. The words "light" and "shower" registered in my mind, and I had my idea.

The original installation now hangs motionless, as if suspended in time, overlooking but not interrupting the view of Loch Ossian. By day it catches glimpses of the sunshine, shedding prismatic flecks of light onto the stairs; by night it morphs into what it is: a shower of light.

Light Shower, *Loch Ossian, Scotland, 2008.*

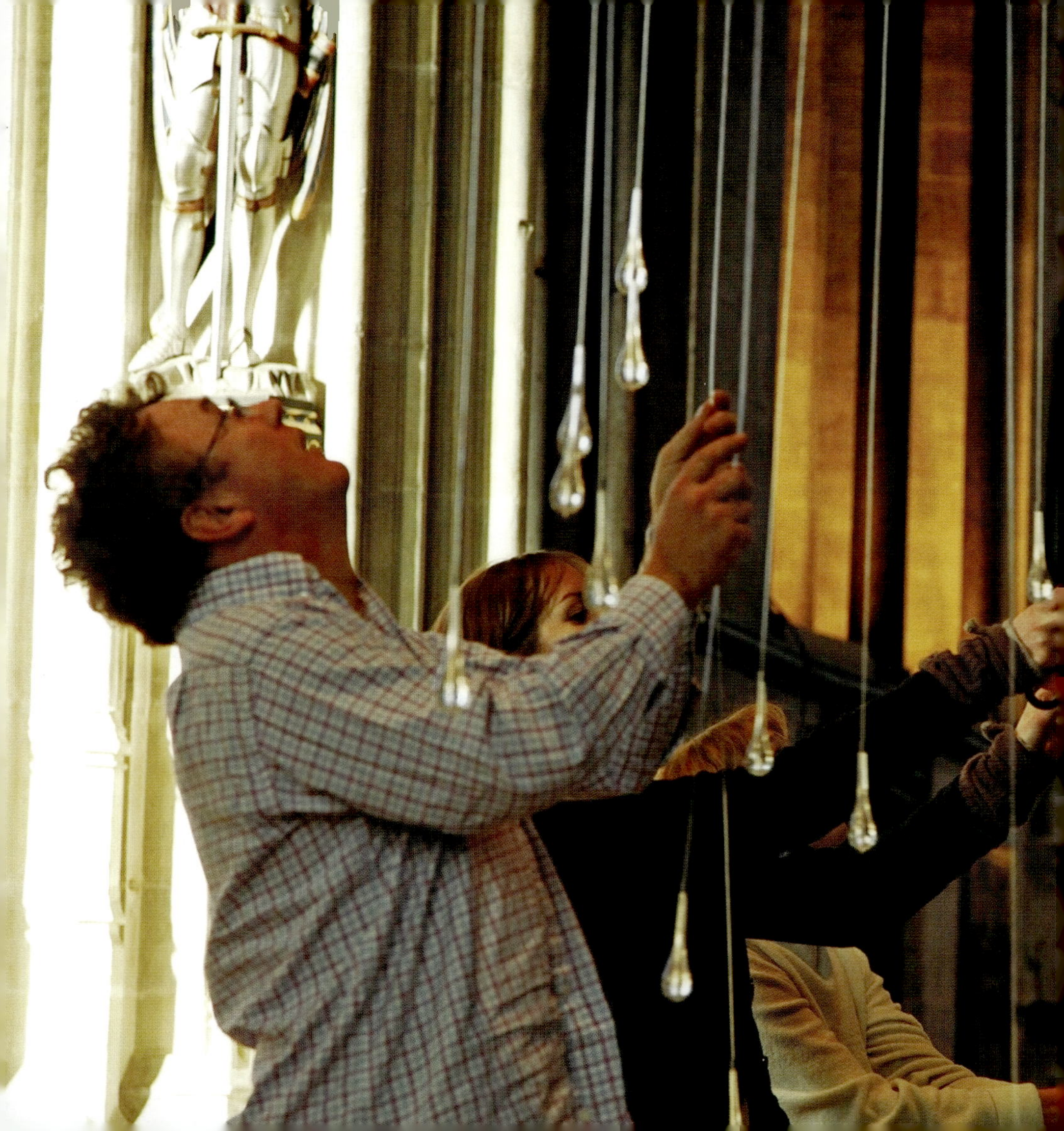

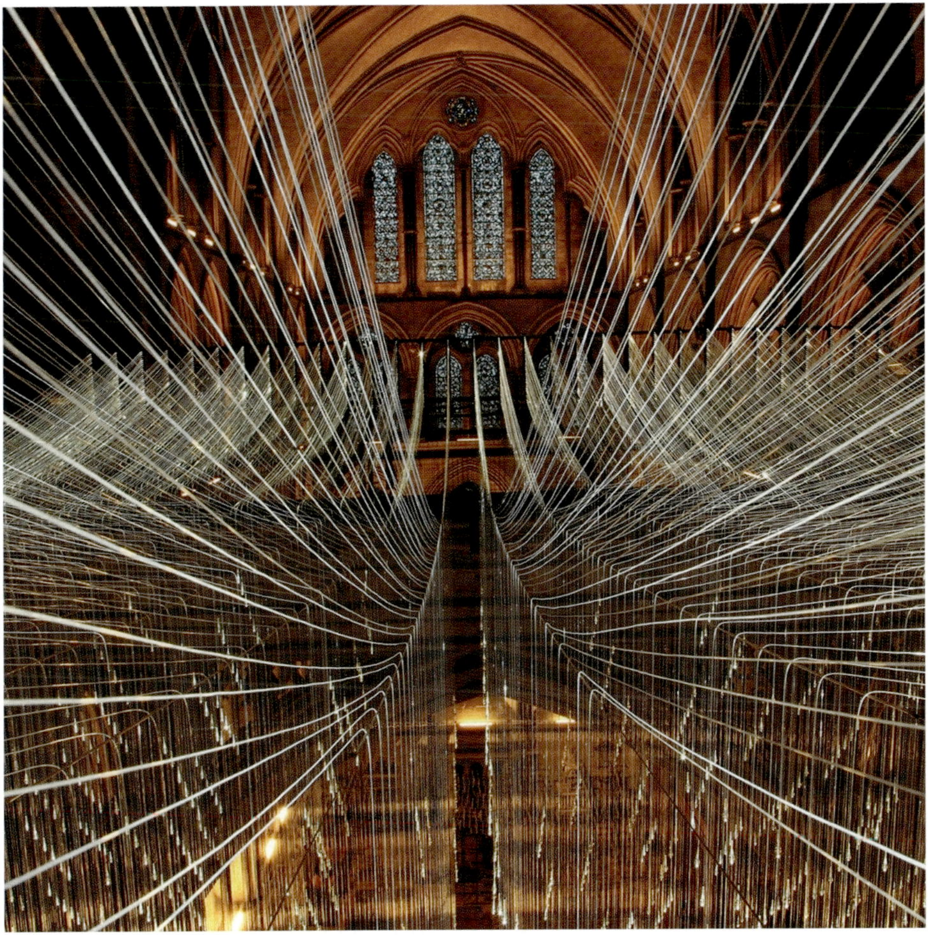

Opposite, above, and over: Light Shower, *Salisbury Cathedral, Wiltshire, UK, 2010.*
Pp. 46–47: Light Shower, *Montalvo Arts Center, Saratoga, California, USA, 2018.*

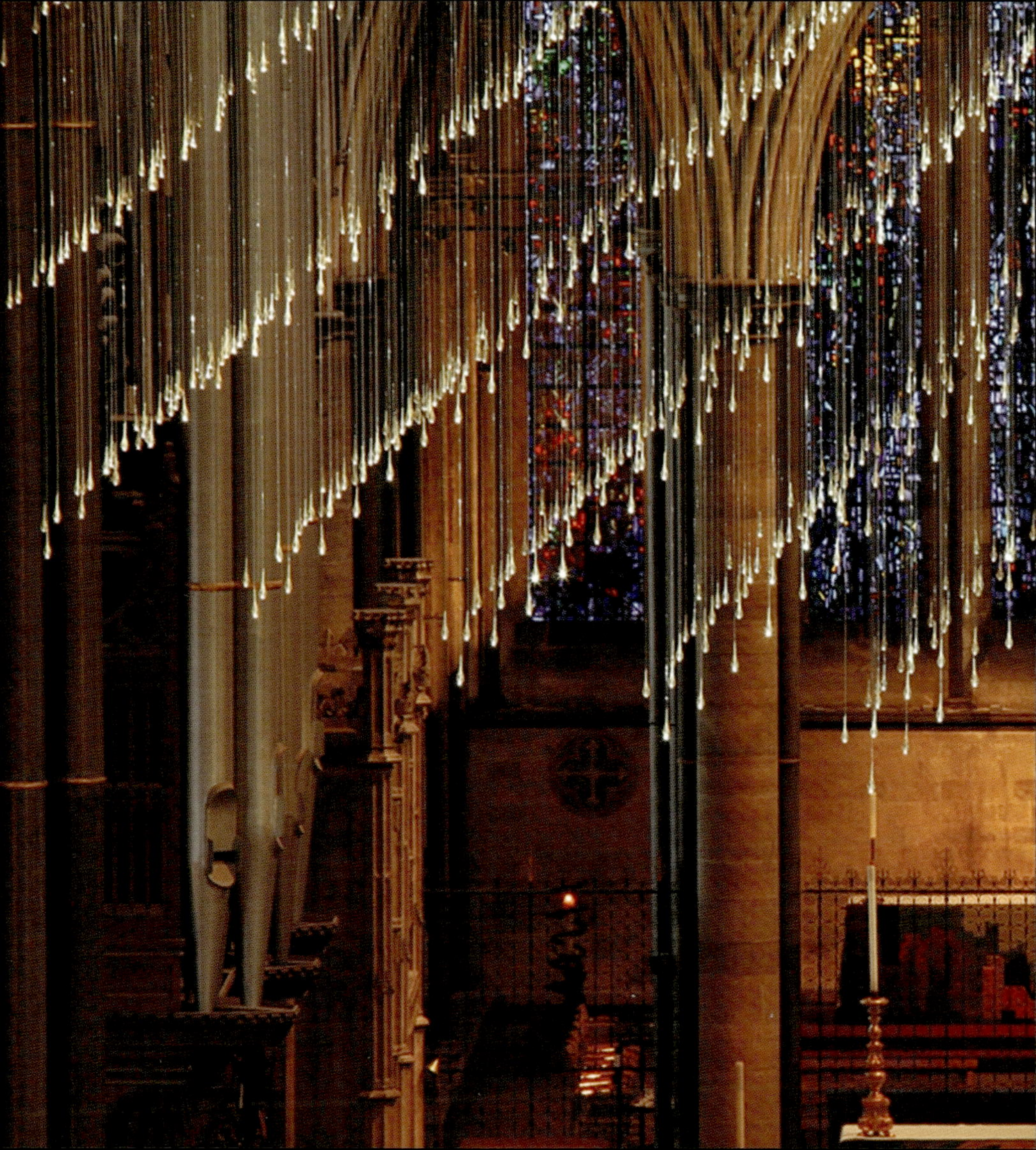

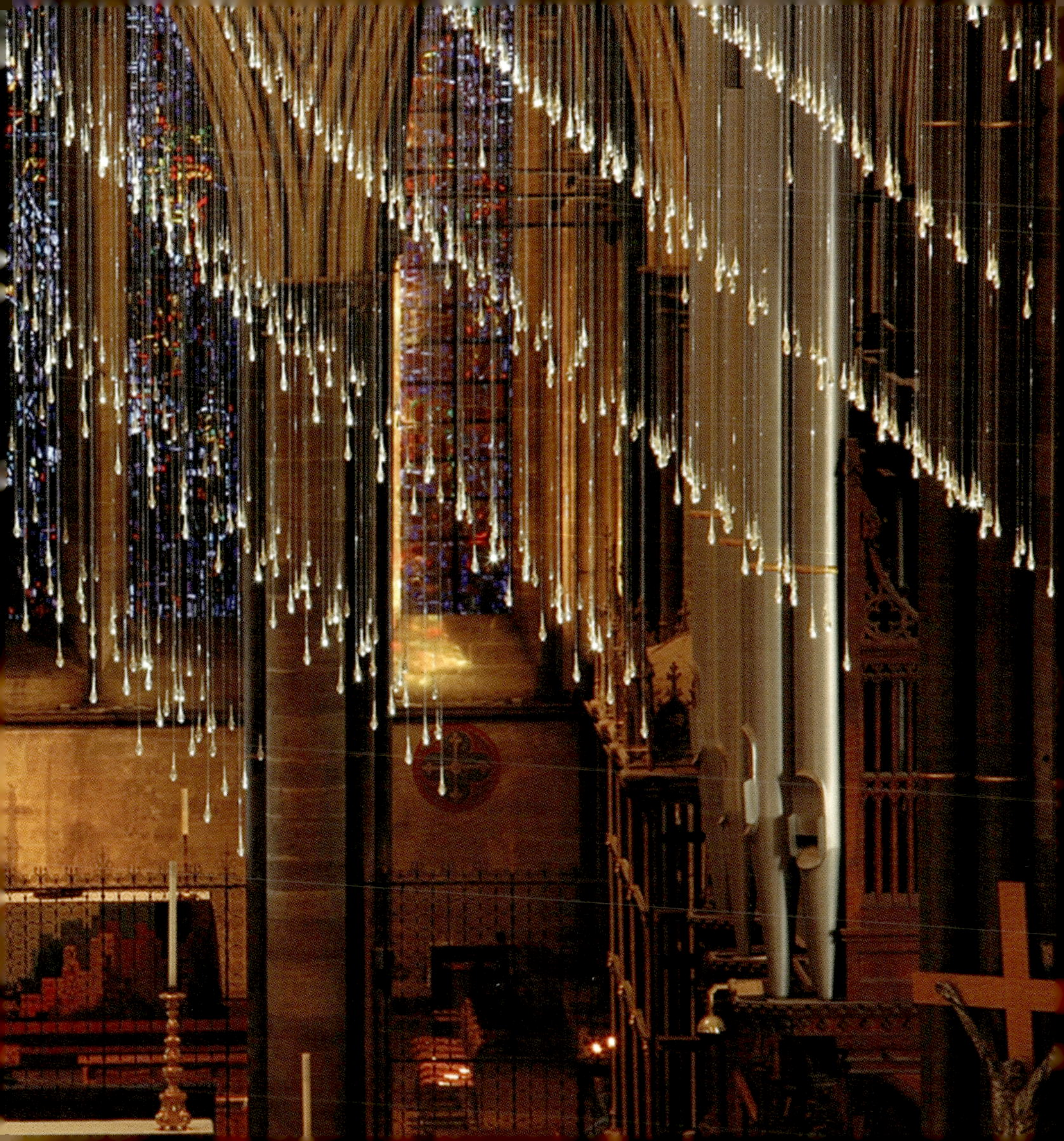

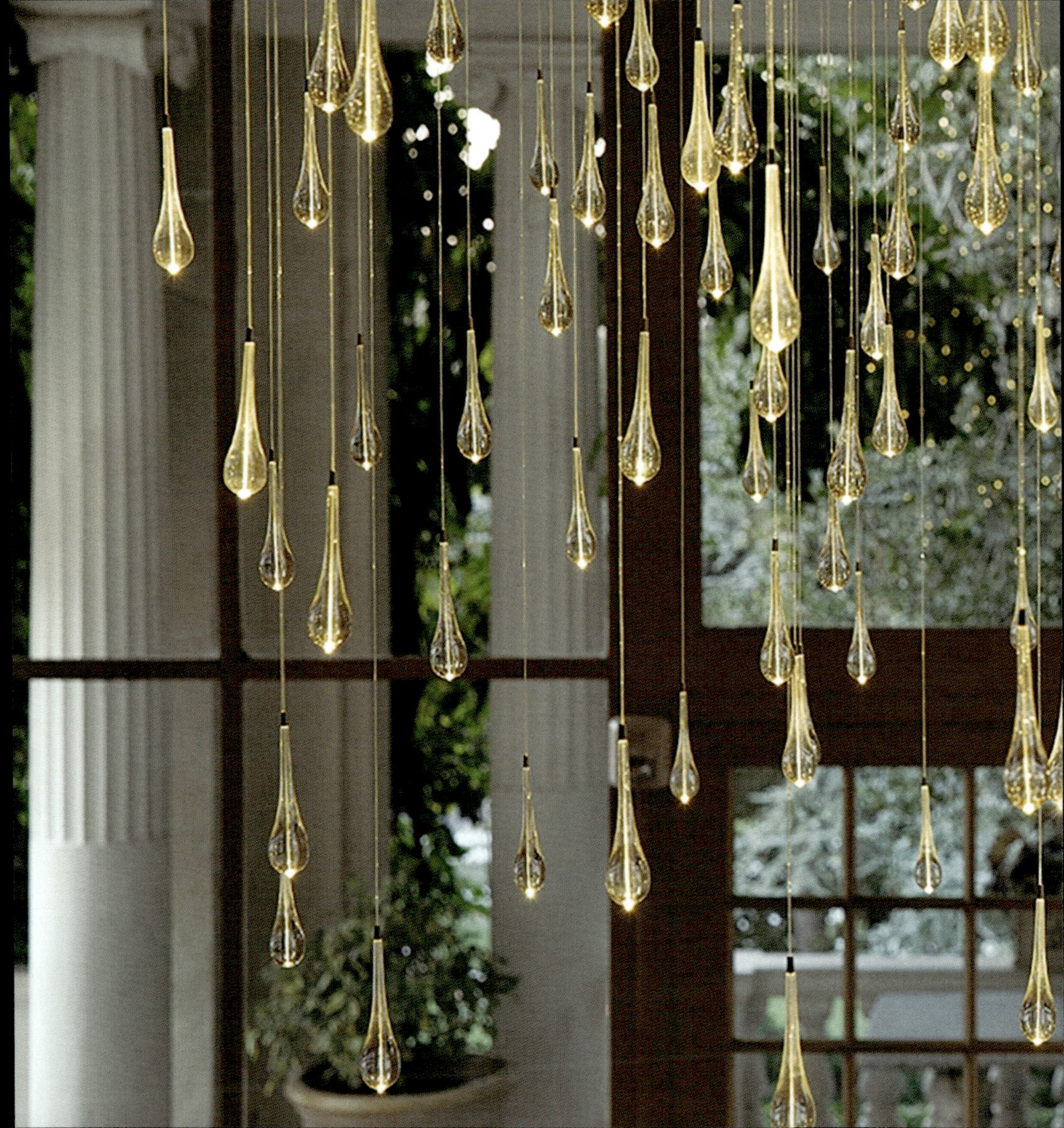

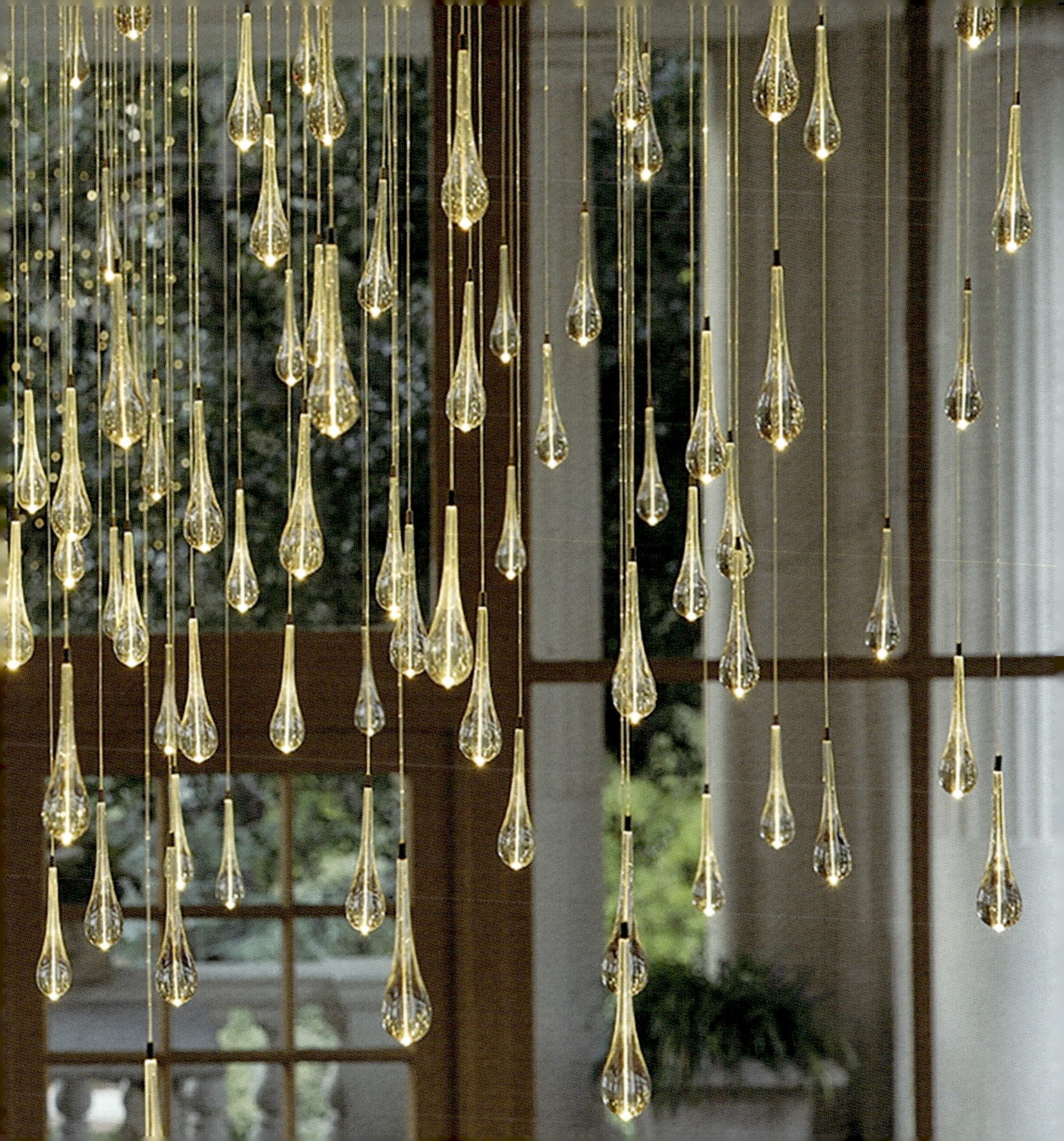

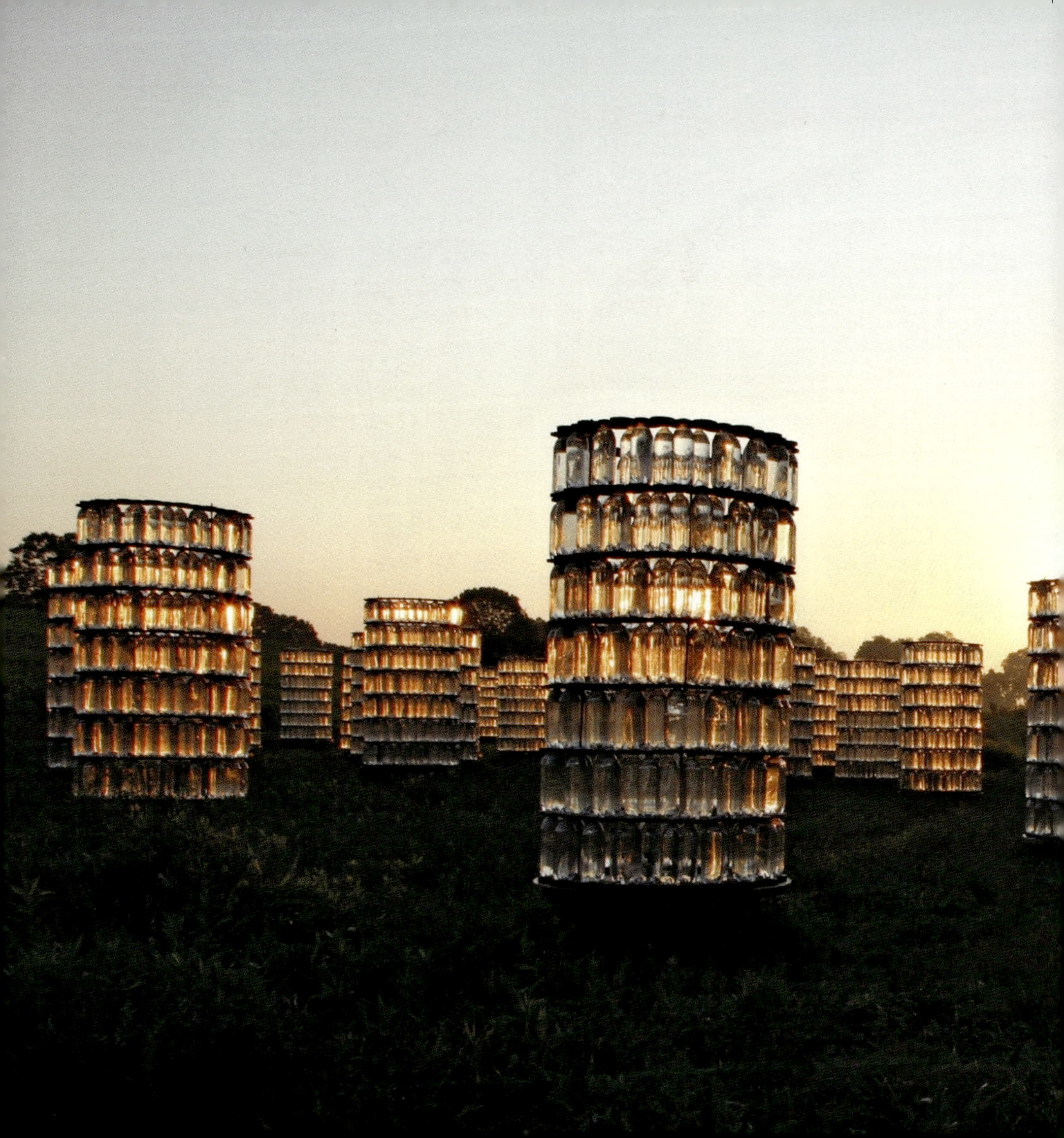

WATER-TOWERS

When I was twenty-one years old, I read a book called *Gifts of Unknown Things* by Lyall Watson, a radical thinker operating on the margins of accepted science. In it, Watson describes Tia, a young girl living on an island in the Indonesian archipelago who possesses the magical gift of seeing sounds in color. Twenty-nine years later, Tia's gift inspired the design for a colorful, watery, musical maze.

Watson described how the Earth has a natural pulse in the upper atmosphere, resonating at a rate of sixty-nine beats per day. The pulse forms a deep note well below human powers of hearing. This Earth pulse inspired *Water-Towers*, which originally consisted of sixty-nine towers; one for each pulse per day. Each tower is about two metres (six feet) tall and made from over 200 stacked water bottles illuminated by optic fibers. In their original formation, the towers resembled enormous liquid batteries of light arranged in a maze formation. Music emanates from the towers; the soundtrack reflects the musical diversity of many nations.

The installation is an exercise in creating something magical from simple materials: PET plastic bottles, laser-cut wooden laminate, and water. A control system scrolls through a rainbow of colors synchronized with the soundtrack. As the towers change color, visitors experience sound magically translated into color, just as Tia, Lyall Watson's heroine, does.

Opposite: Water-Towers, *Longwood Gardens, Pennsylvania, USA, 2012.*
Pp. 50–51: Water-Towers, *Desert Botanical Garden, Arizona , USA, 2015.*
Pp. 52–53: Water-Towers, *Light Art Festa, Jeju, South Korea, 2018.*
Pp. 54–55: Water-Towers, *Tropical Light, Darwin, Northern Territory, Australia, 2020.*

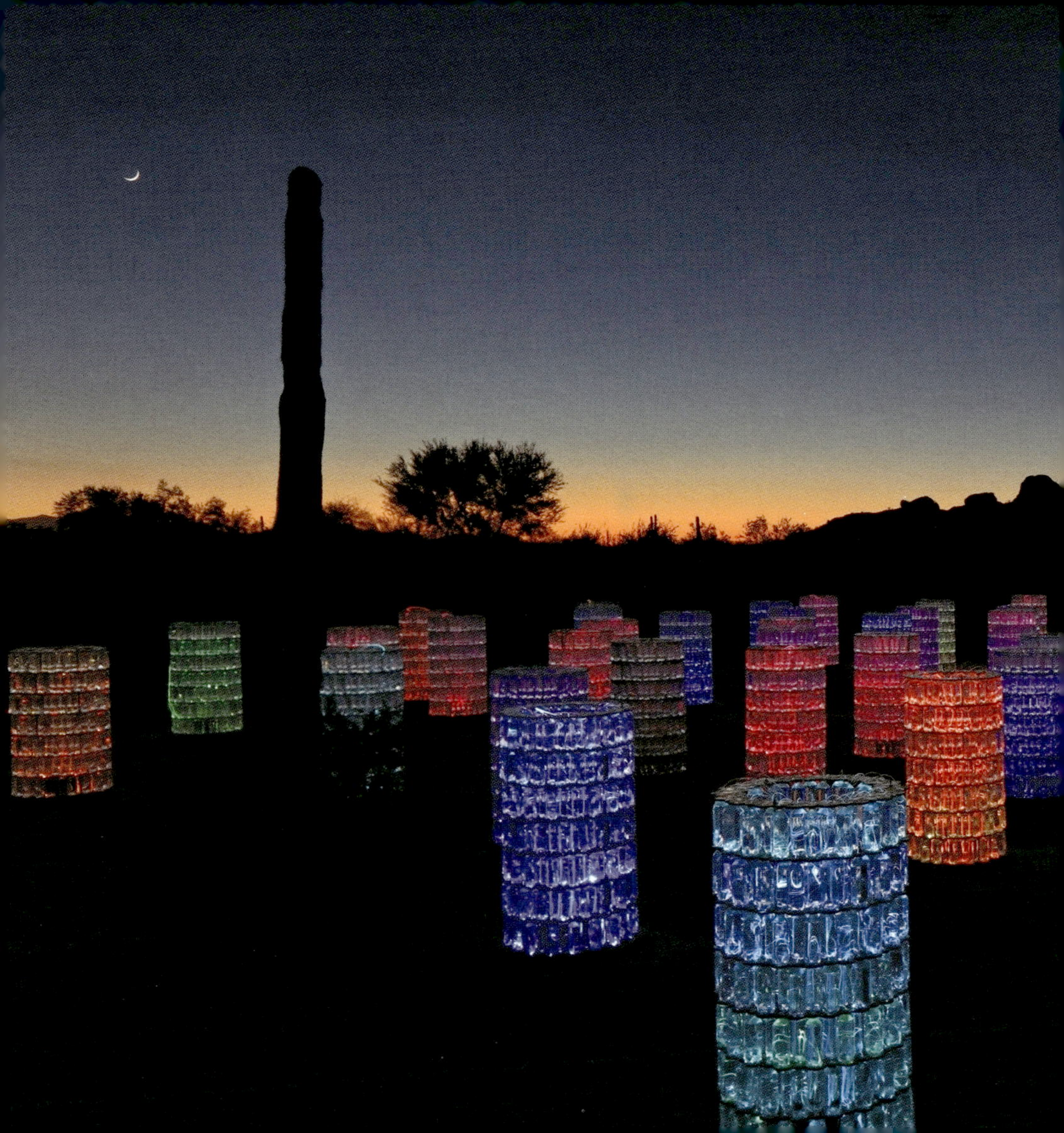

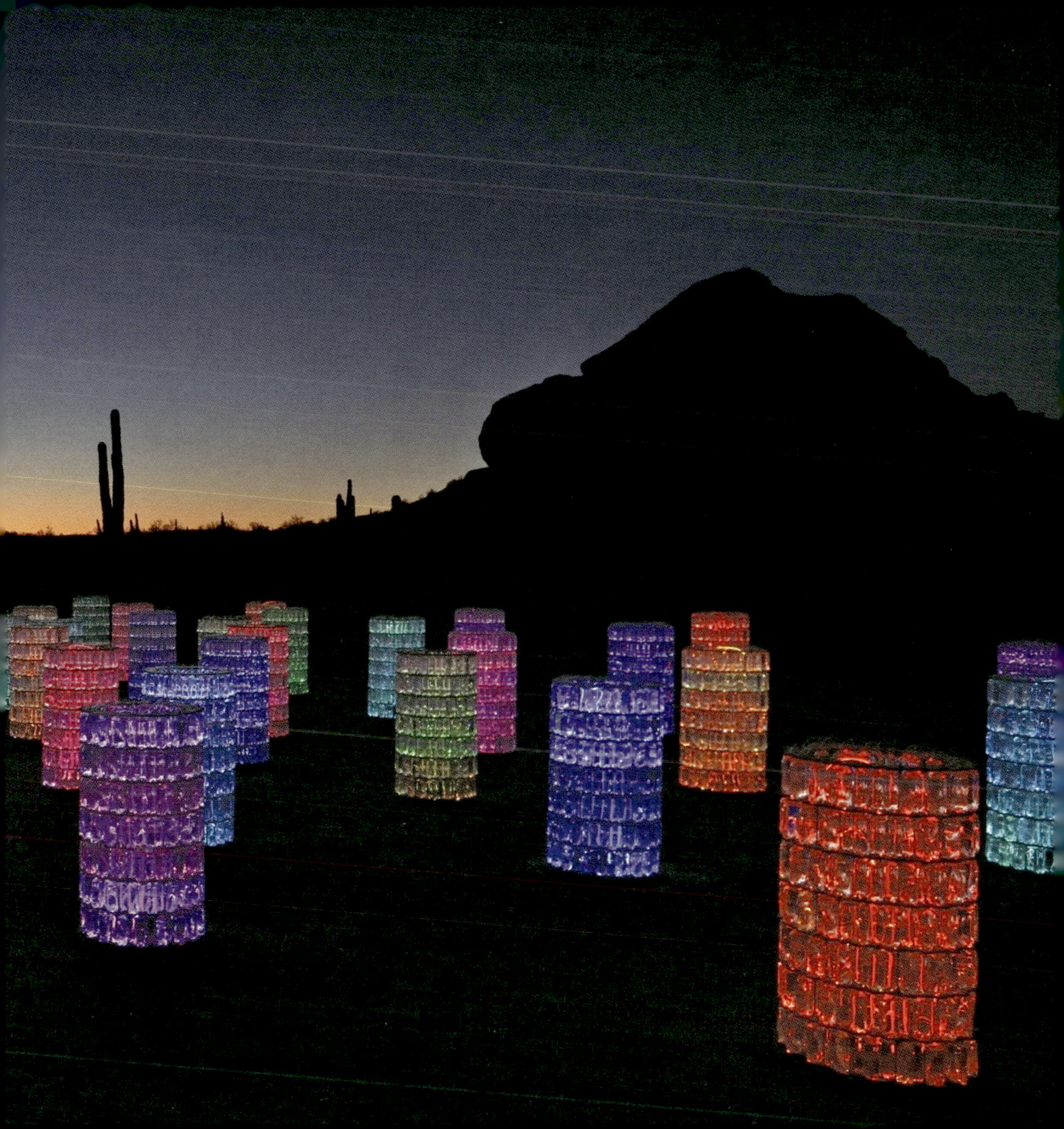

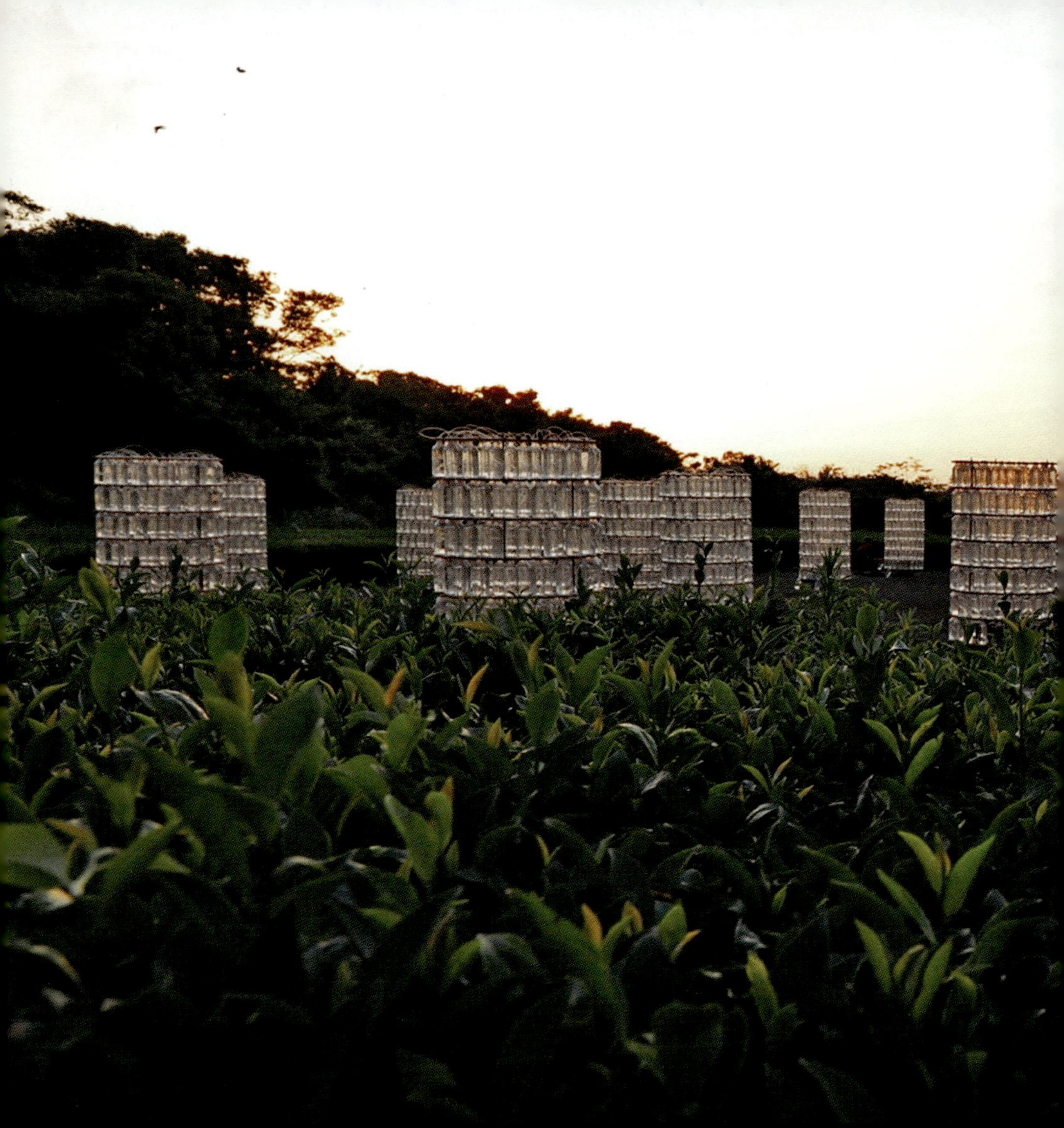

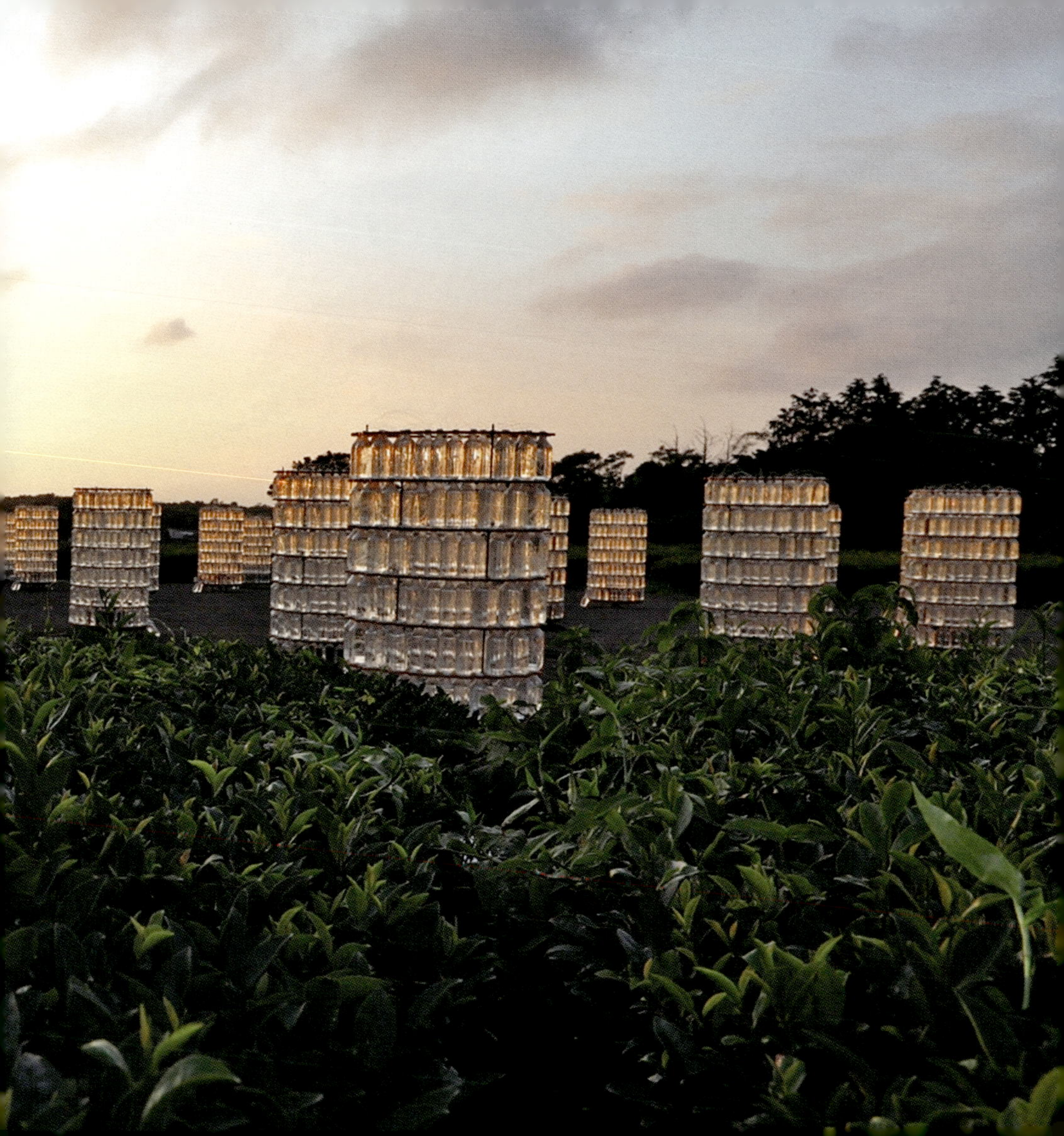

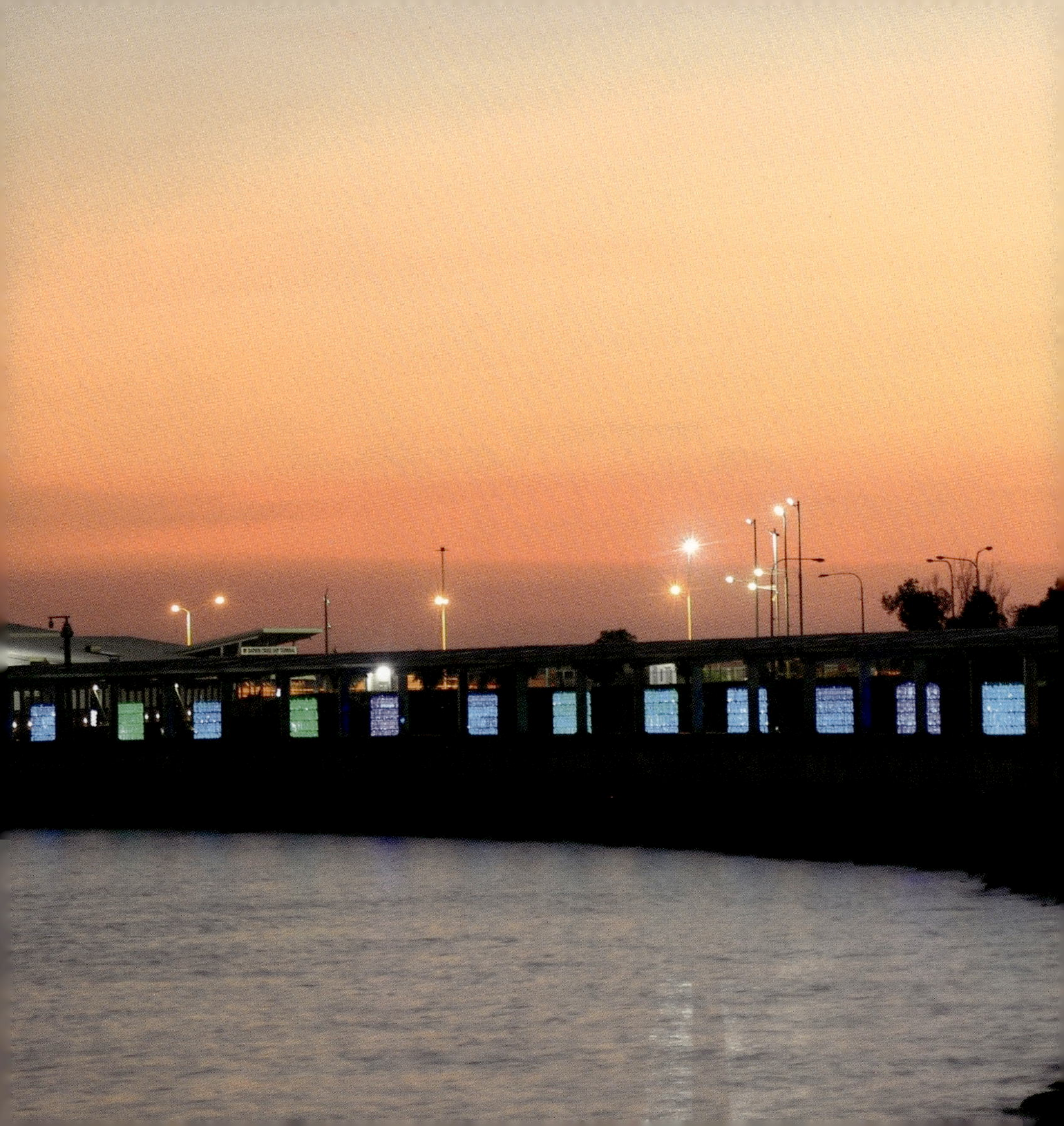

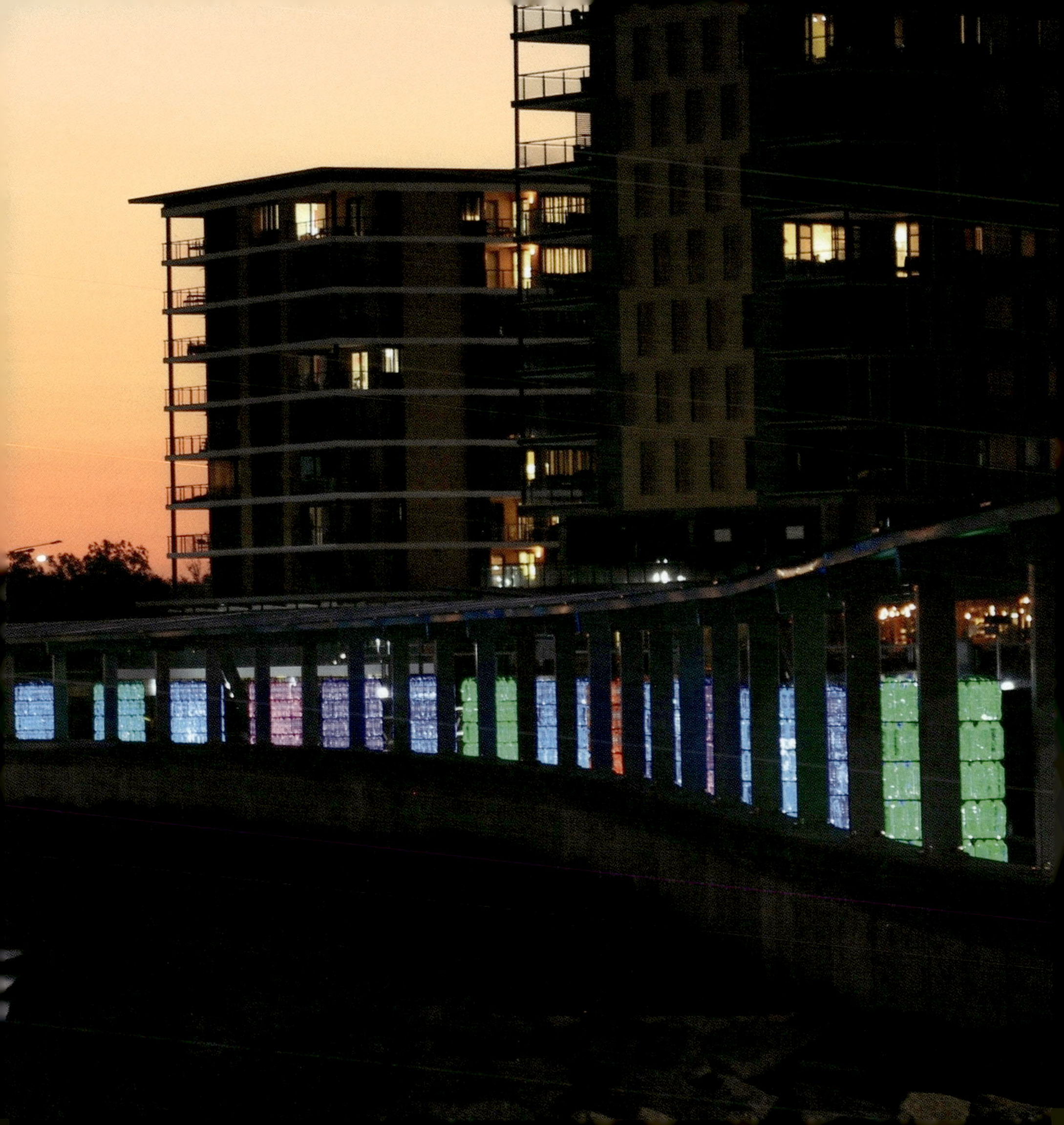

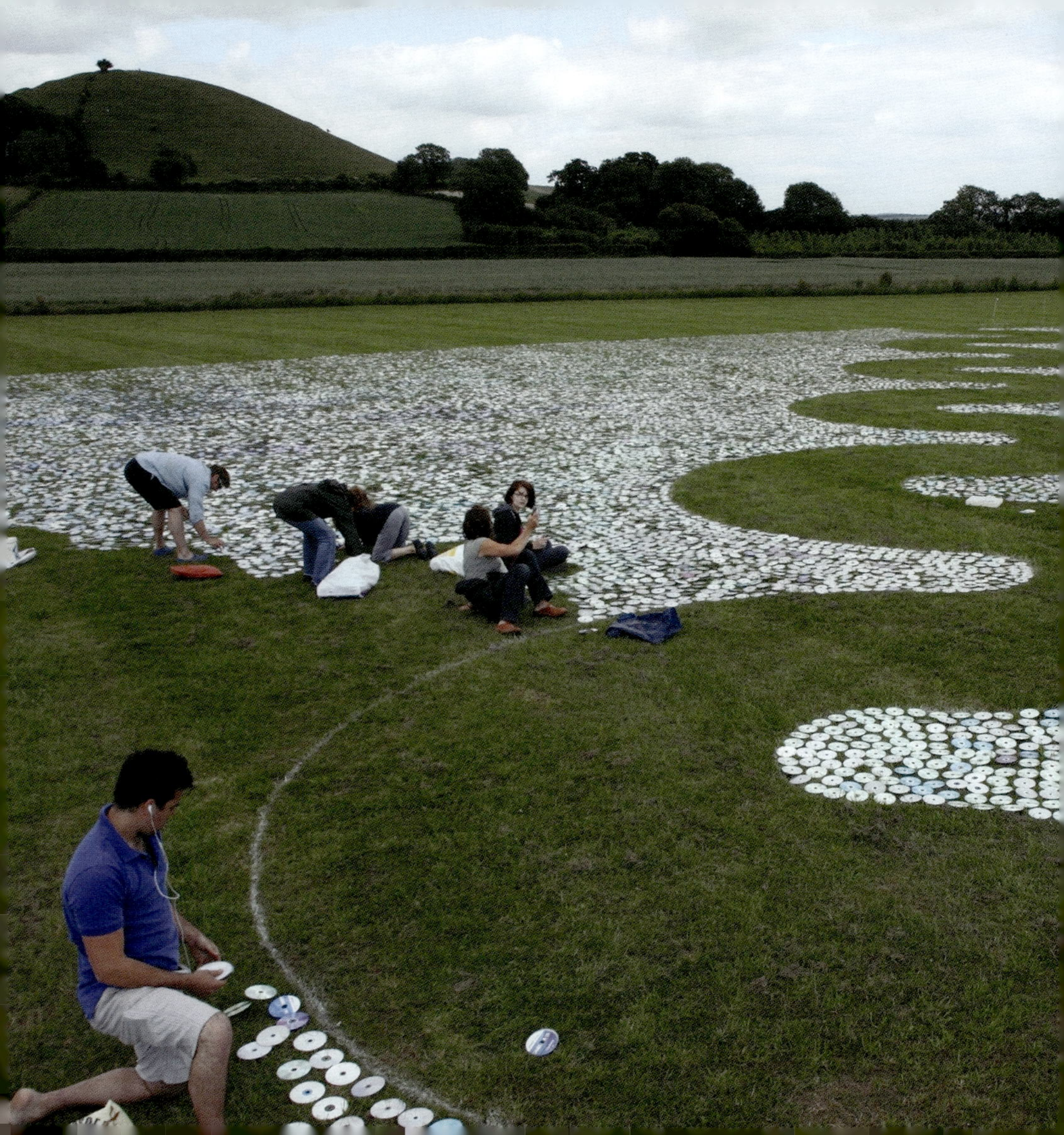

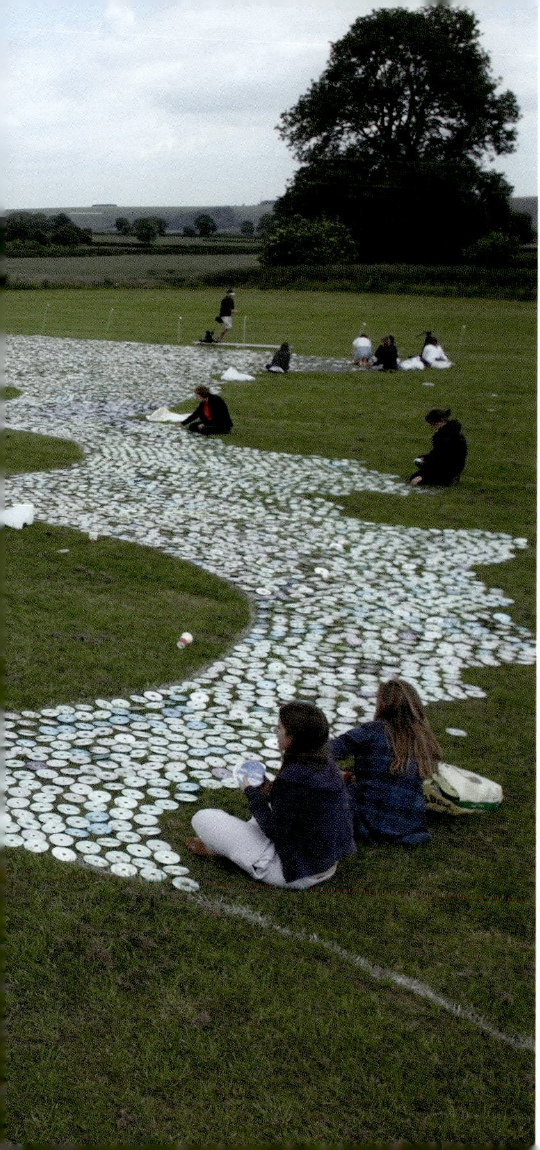

CDSEA

Entitled *CDSea*, this project was installed in June 2010 at Long Knoll Field in Wiltshire, where in 2004 we installed a prototype of the *Field of Light*. A public footpath intersects the field, and this meant that *CDSea* was on public view from the moment it was installed. Personal friends and family, including families with young children, all helped me and my team install *CDSea*.

CDSea is literally an inland sea created from 600,000 discarded compact discs, which were donated from all around the world. They created a carpet of glinting light, created by the reflections of the solstice sun. As with the *Field of Light*, the catalyst for *CDSea* was living in Australia, where eight years of exposure to the Antipodean sun left a lasting impression on me. *CDSea* was inspired one Sunday afternoon as I was sitting on a rocky

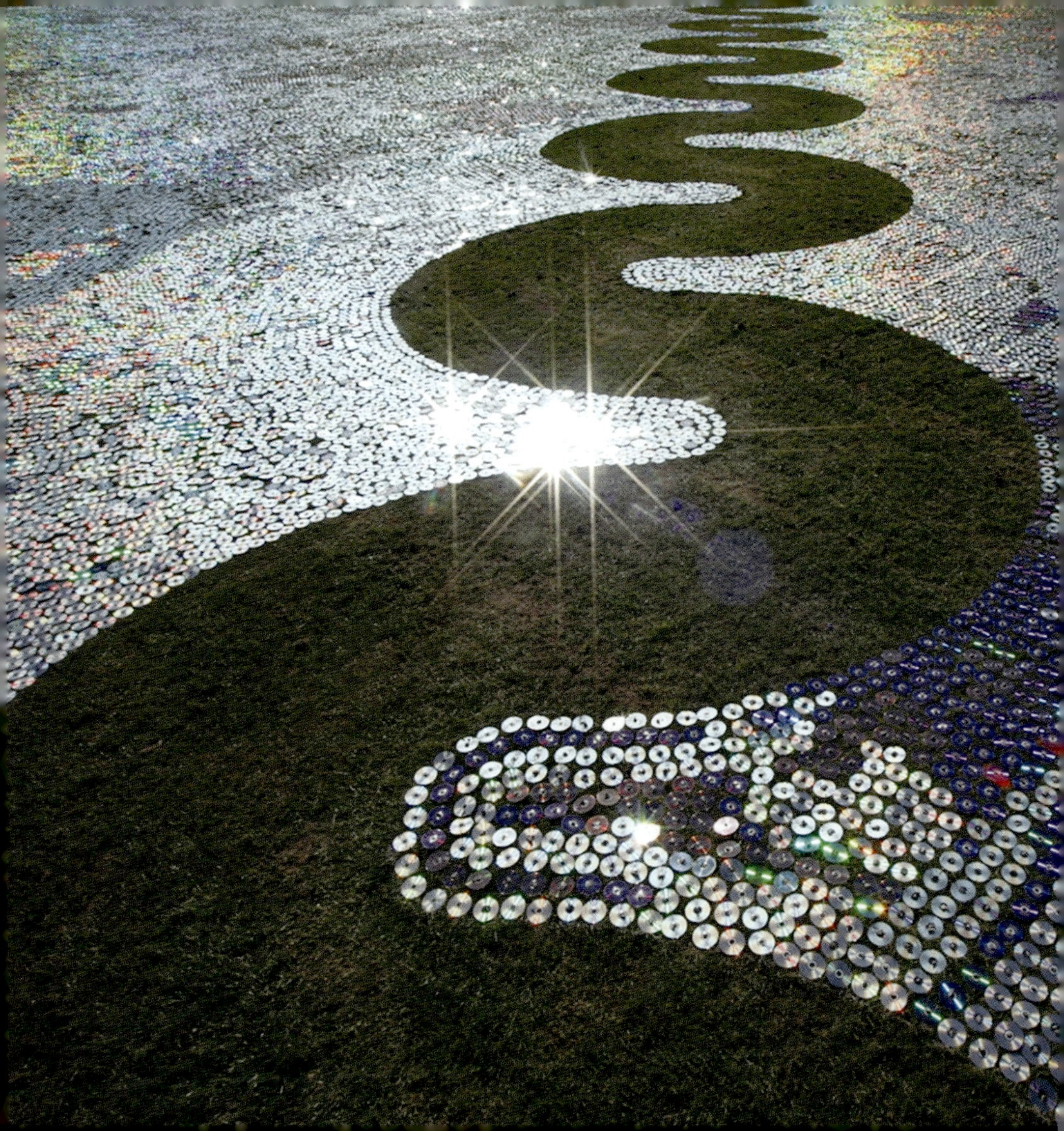

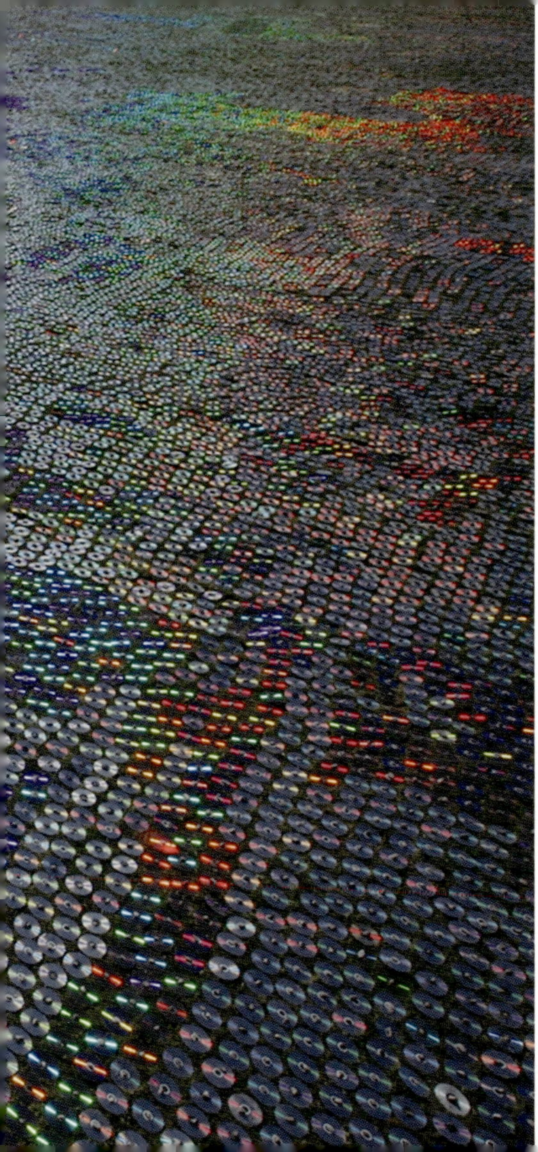

peninsula at Nielsen Park, one of the beautiful Sydney Harbour beaches, where I would go when I was a bit down or in the dumps. The light was still strong, like a blanket of shimmering silver light. I had this childish notion that by putting my hand in the sea I was somehow connected to my home in Salcombe, South Devon, where my father lived. I came away from the beach in a very positive at-one-with-the-world frame of mind. It was the first time I was aware that the play of light had transformed my mood, and it proved an unforgettable turning point in my life. I was astonished that something so familiar had the power to alter my emotional state. *CDSea* is a reconstruction of this event.

I do not expect visitors to feel exactly as I did, but I am certain that the materials, scale, and location, a field on top of a hill, will evoke emotions unique to each observer. If it inspires some smiling faces, then the emotional force has been successfully passed on.

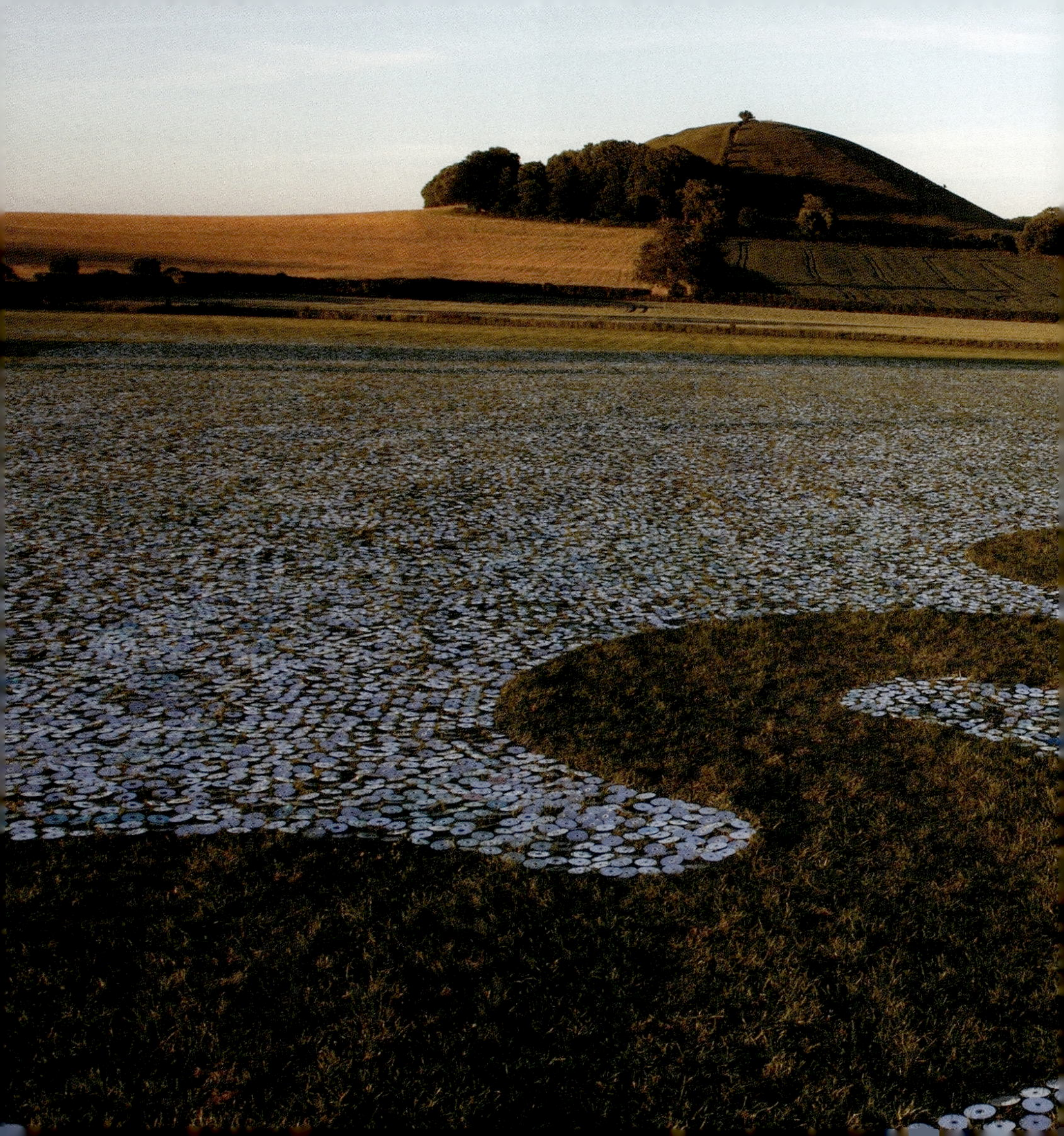

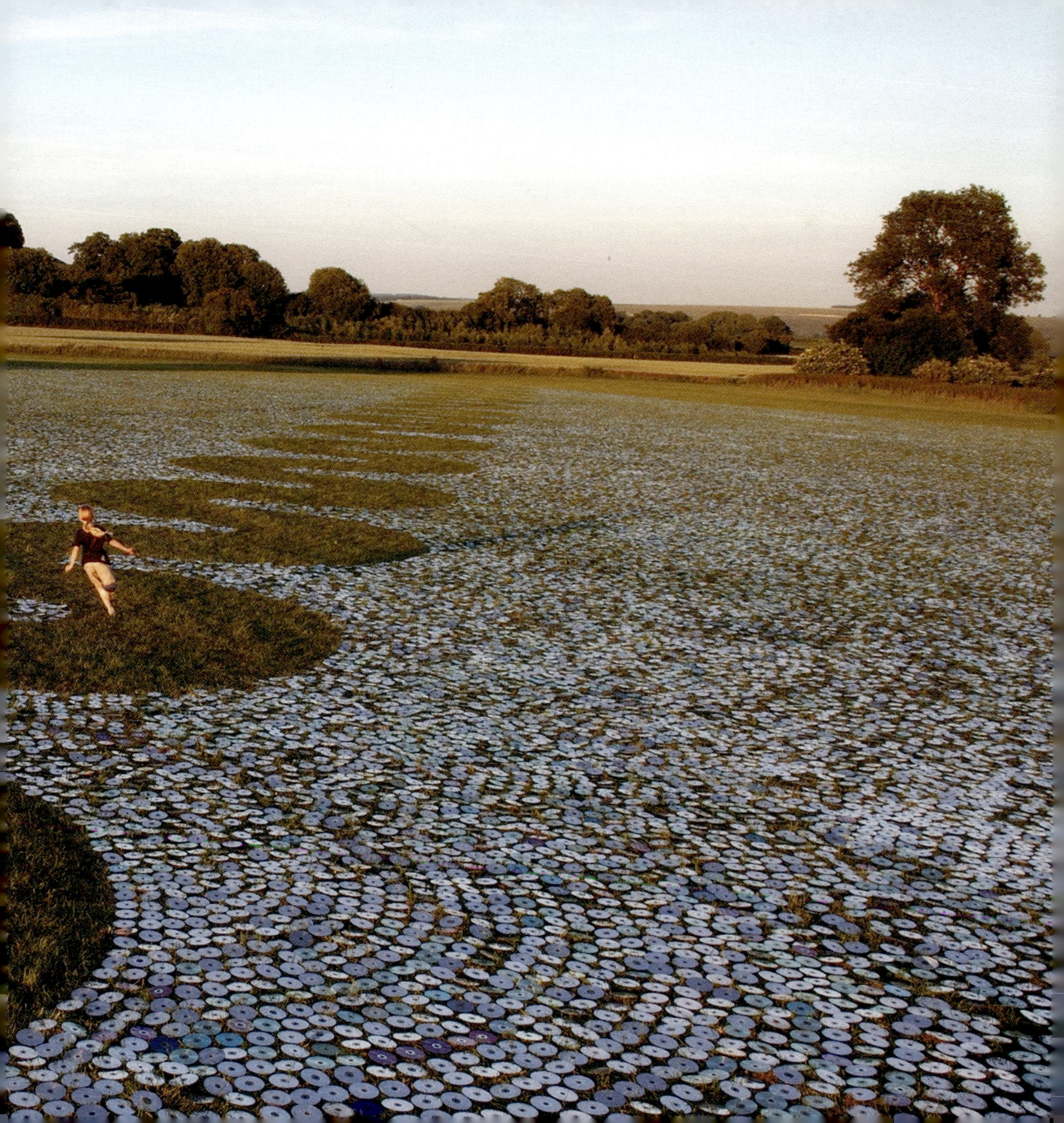

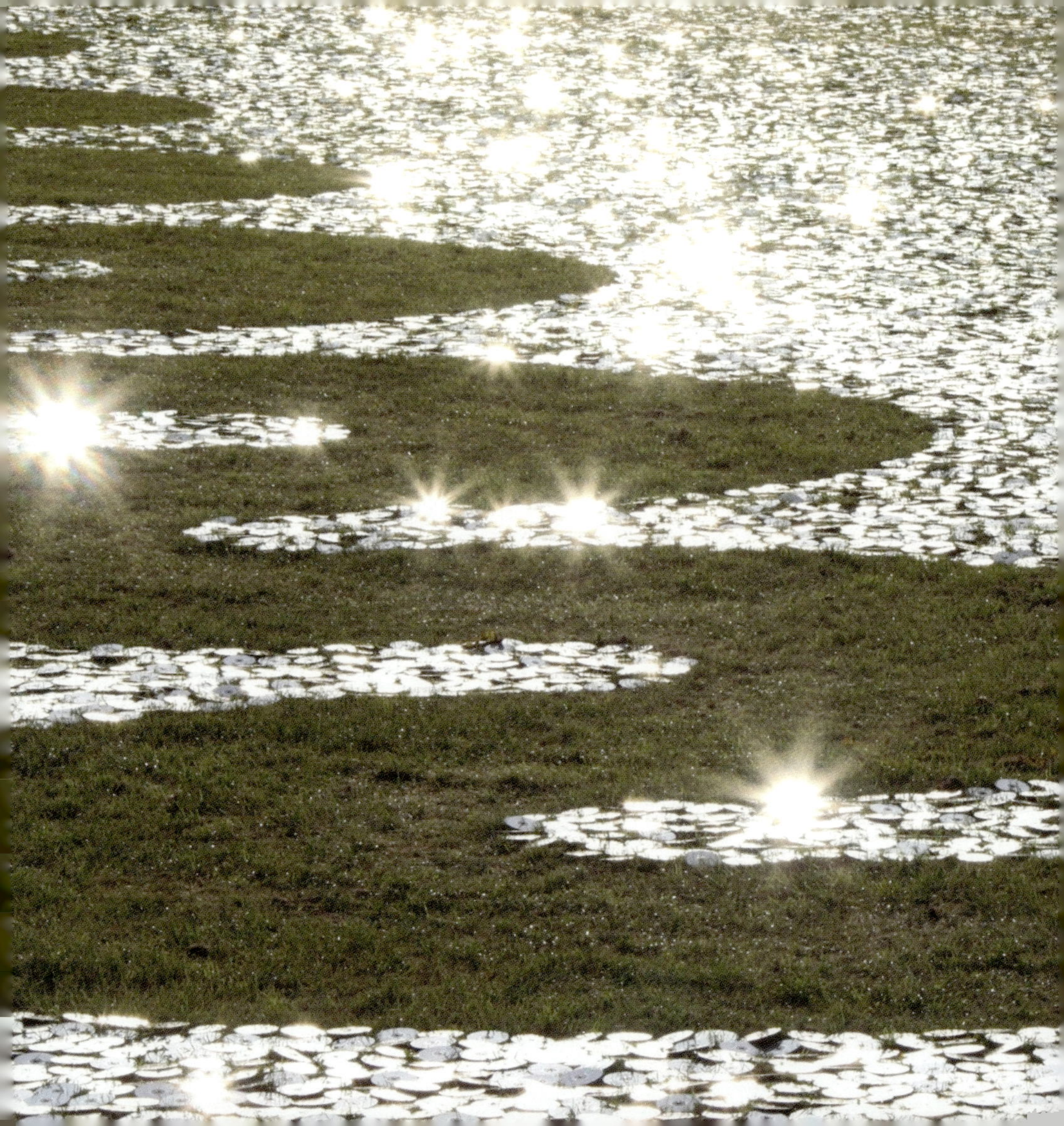

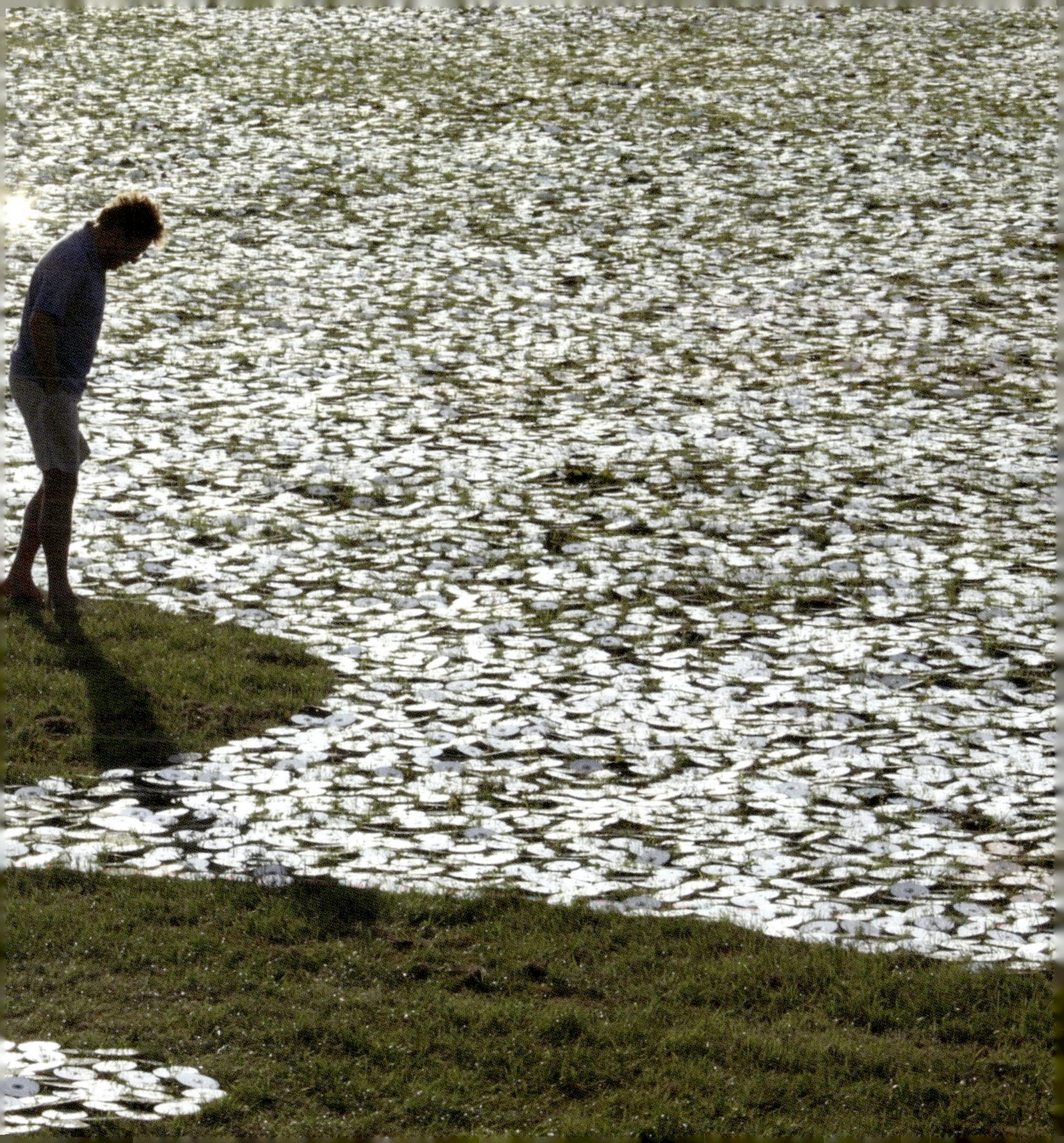

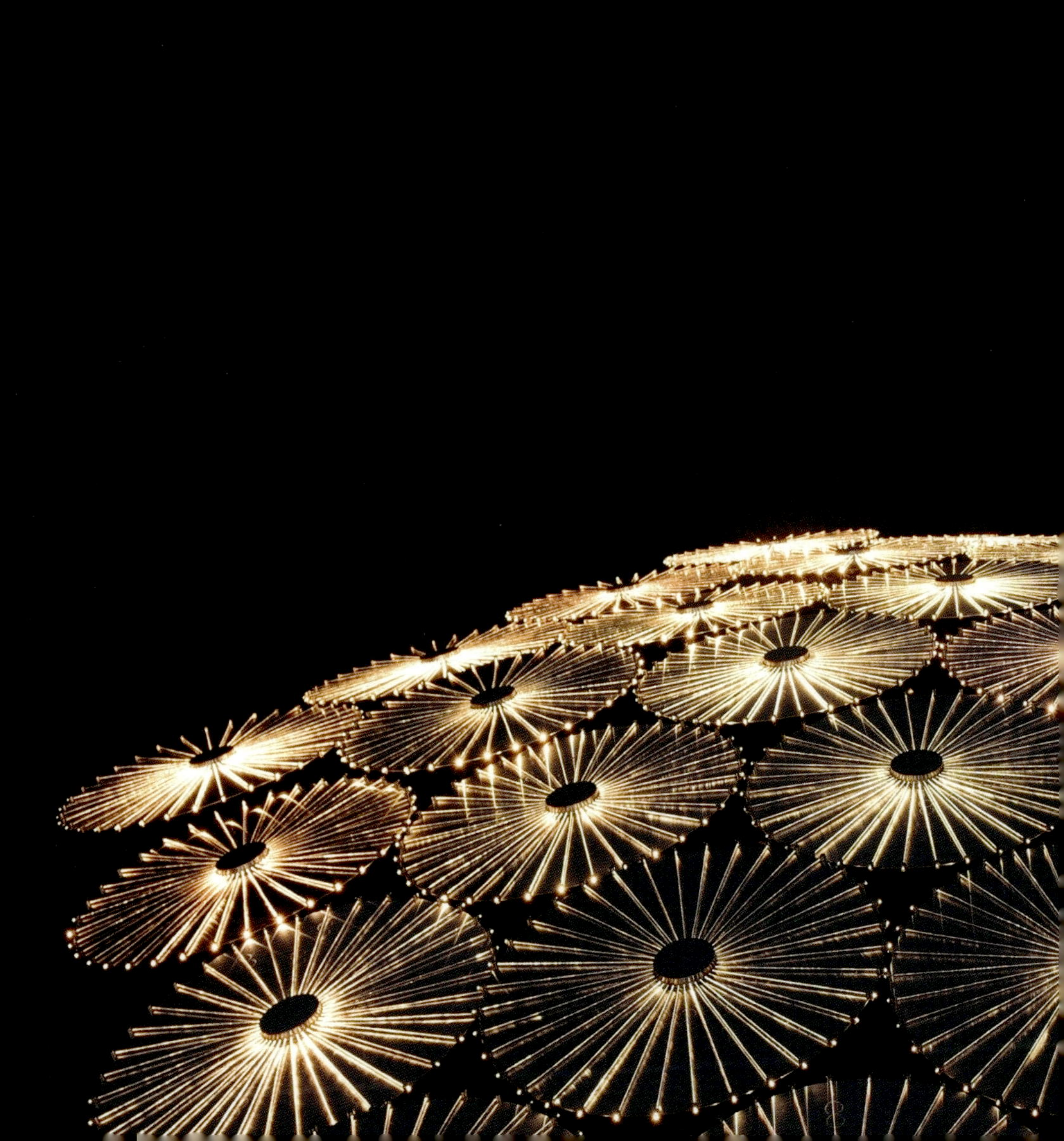

SOUTHERN LIGHT

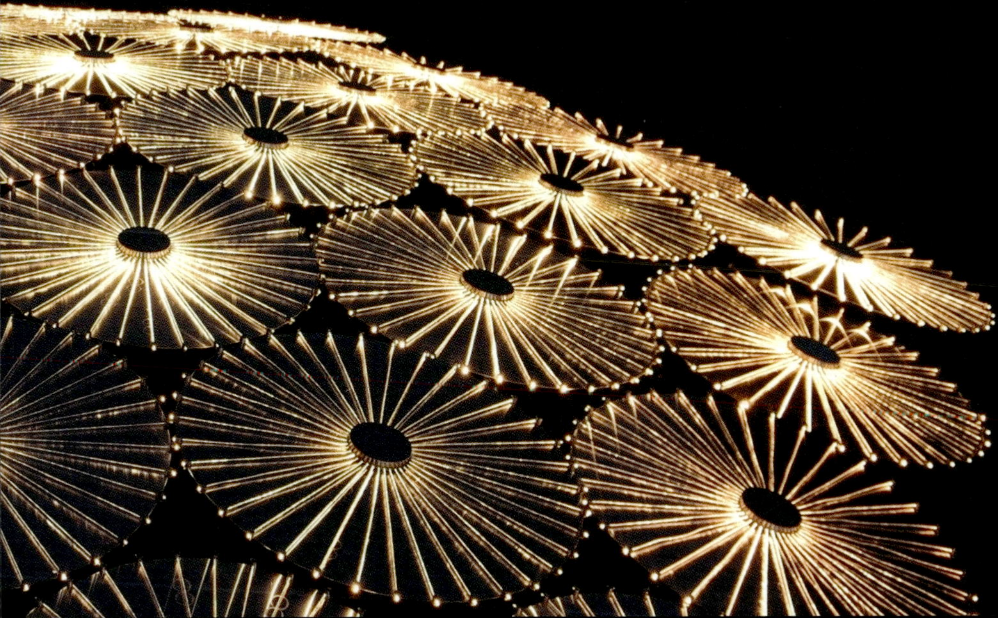

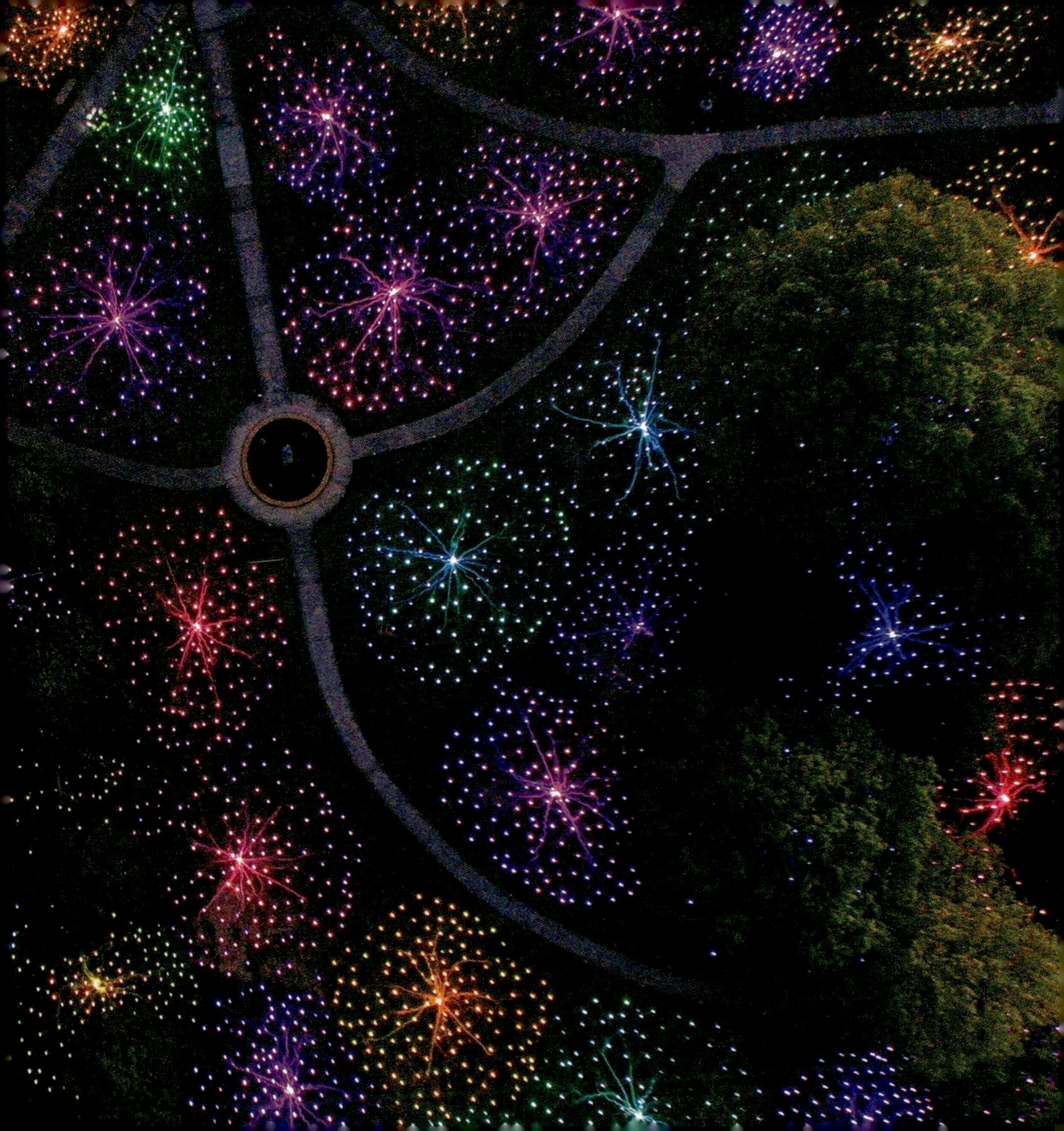

EXHIBITION STATEMENT

BRUCE MUNRO

My first visit to a potential exhibition site sets the tone for the artwork that will follow. Time is of the essence as there is often a great deal to see. My approach is always the same: I place my mind into neutral gear and explore the spaces, often with the aid of a plan or map, simply allowing my eyes and imagination to wonder and dream.

During my site visit to Brookgreen Gardens in August of 2018, I was impressed by the notion of a garden made from a series of interconnected outside rooms, and that these carefully cultivated "garden rooms" populated by figurative sculptures were surrounded by an untamed landscape. Brookgreen is an extraordinary place with an edge of the unknown! It has been both a pleasure and honor to bring to fruition an exhibition of installations at Brookgreen Gardens.

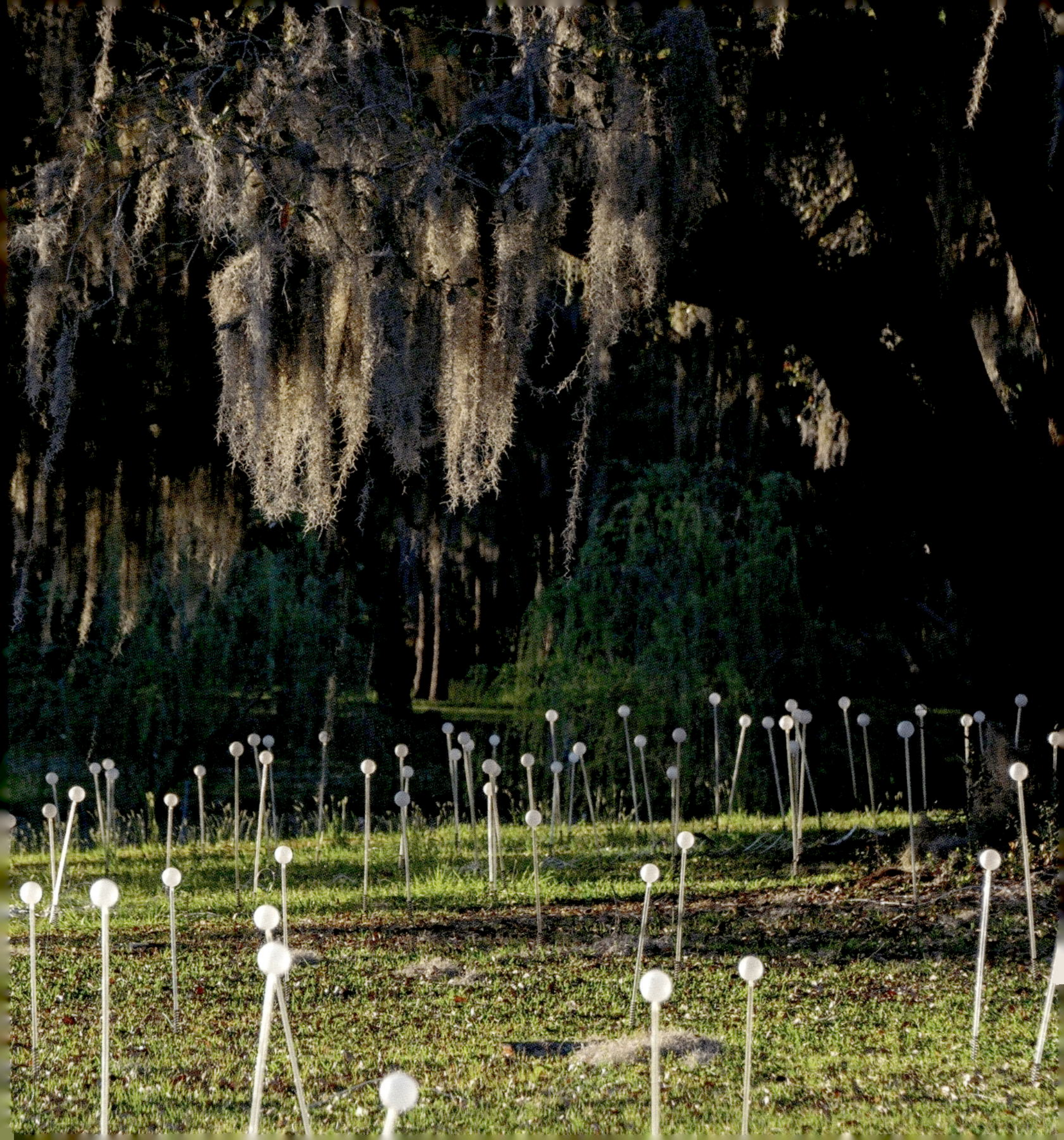

FIELD OF LIGHT

2004–2020; mixed media (acrylic, stainless steel, fiber optics, frosted glass, light source)

The *Field of Light* installation was one idea that stubbornly stayed lodged in my mind over the succeeding years, but I didn't have any opportunity to make a large version until 2004, in the field behind my house in rural Wiltshire. We left it up for a year to test it. People began popping over at odd times to visit it, and that's when I began to realize its effect.

Field of Light seems to inspire many thoughts and ideas. It brings people together, and most importantly, makes people smile—a worthy epitaph for a moment of inspiration in life's journey.

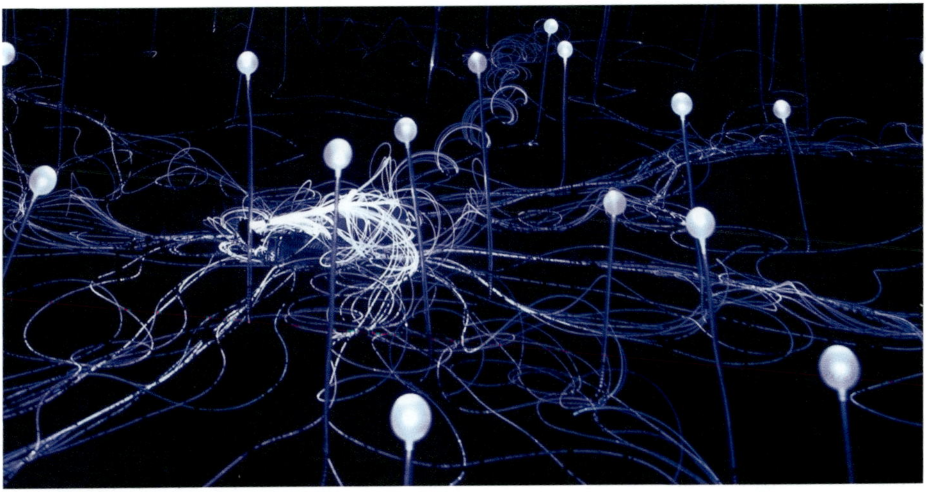

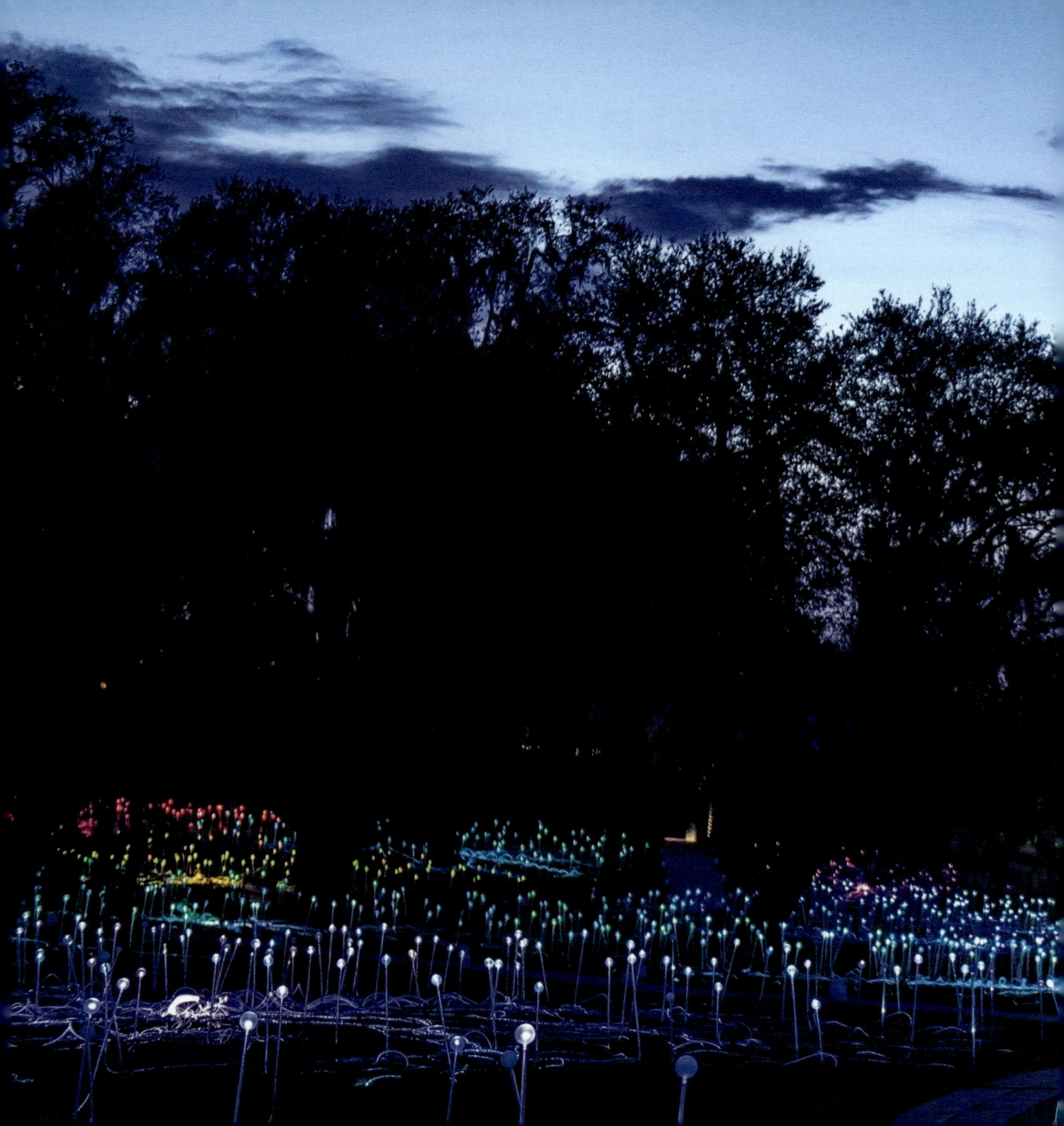

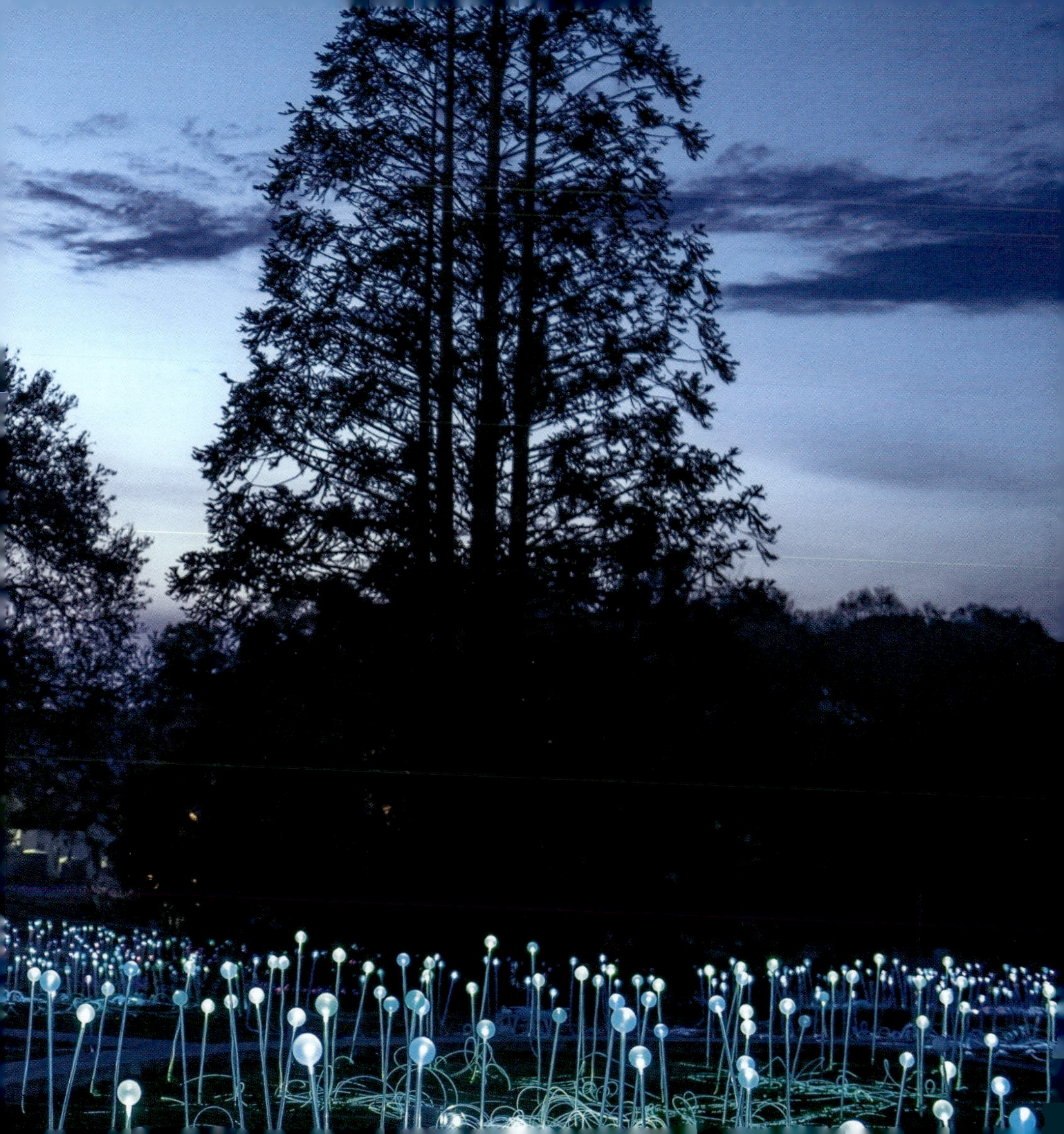

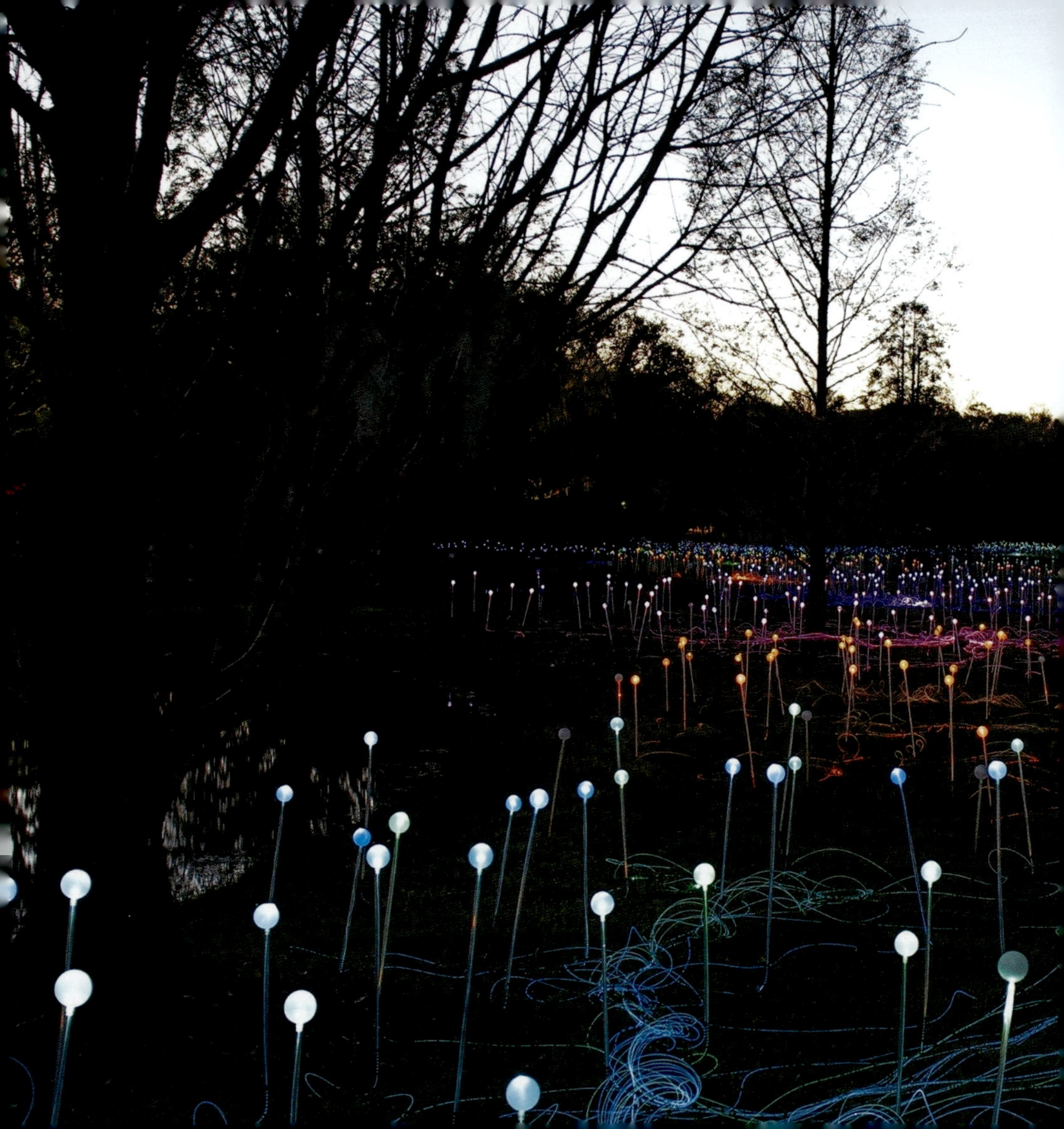

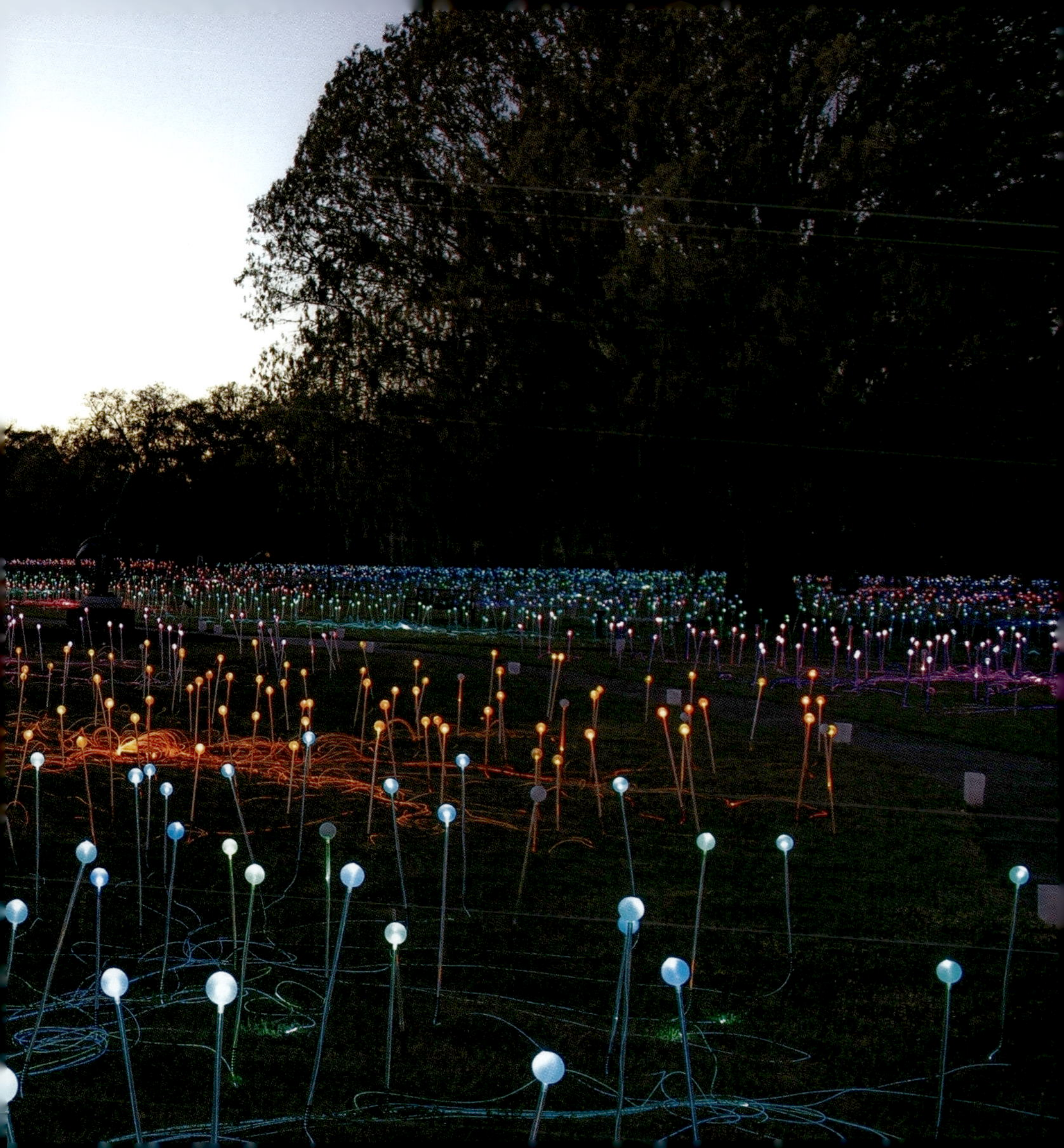

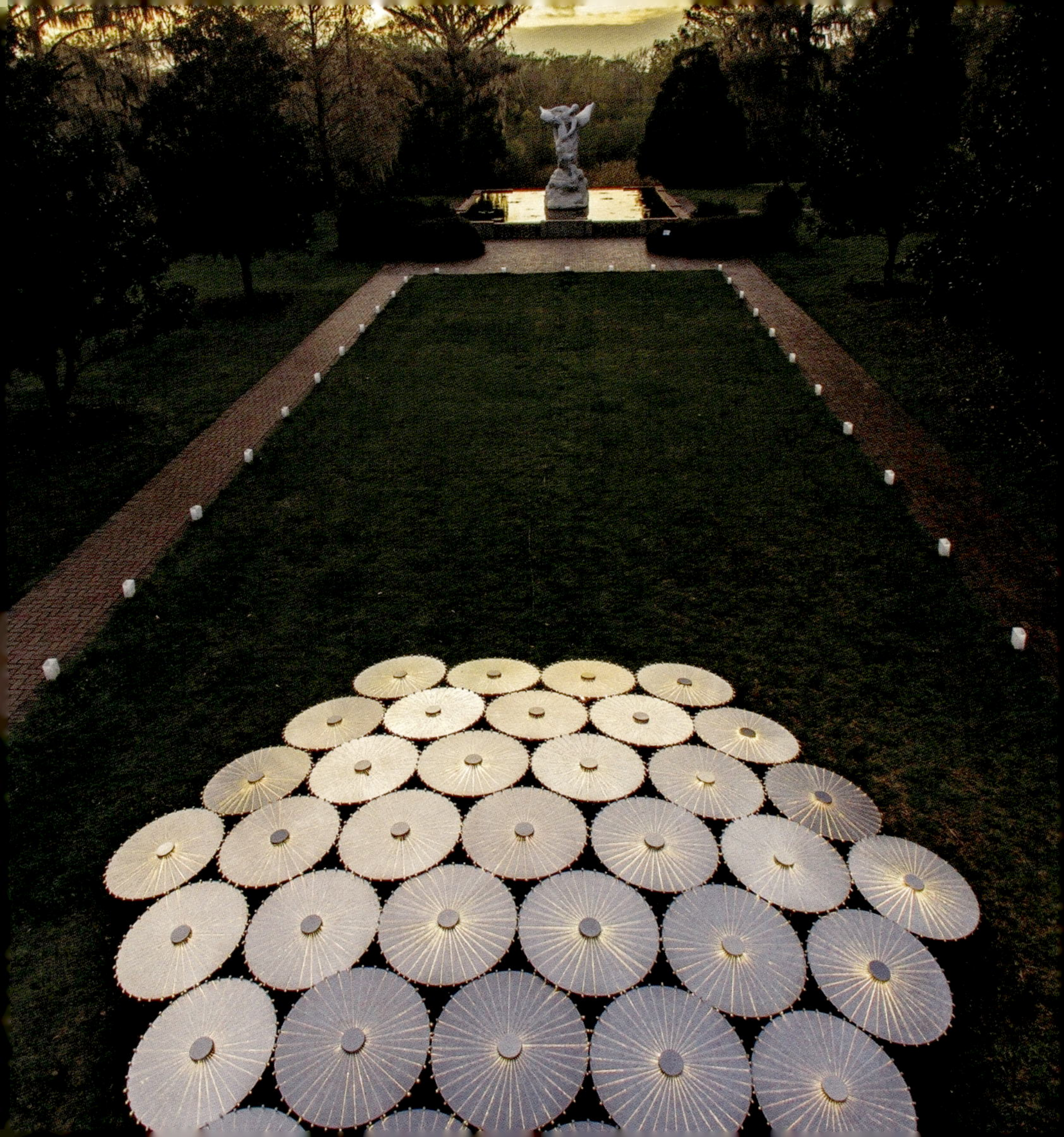

TIME AND AGAIN

2016–2020; mixed media (stainless steel, fiber optics , light source)

Time and Again follows my interest in time and how we move through it. It is a work in progress, an amalgam of the time-based installations that I have created to date.

In 2016, I was able to complete a dream project for a *Field of Light* at Uluṟu (Ayer's Rock), Australia, the place that had inspired it twenty-five years earlier. I realized the great rock had not changed a bit in twenty-five years, yet I had changed a great deal. That experience led to the creation of a set of steel "lilies" marked with a time-code pattern, a design I devised to indicate that present time is linked to a significant past and an undefined future.

The installation at Brookgreen Gardens takes the form of a mythical timepiece, replacing our normal ideals of time with the concept of one eternal timeless moment. By day the installation lies dormant, quietly marking time of the clouds and sky. By night the central hub of each lily shimmers with radial starbursts of light.

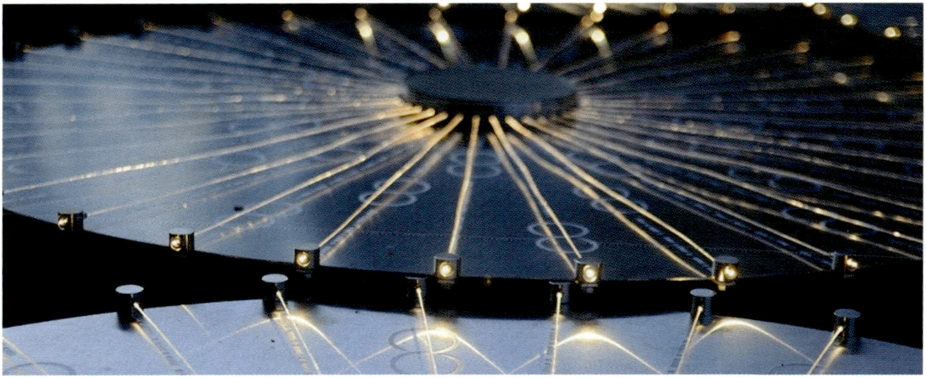

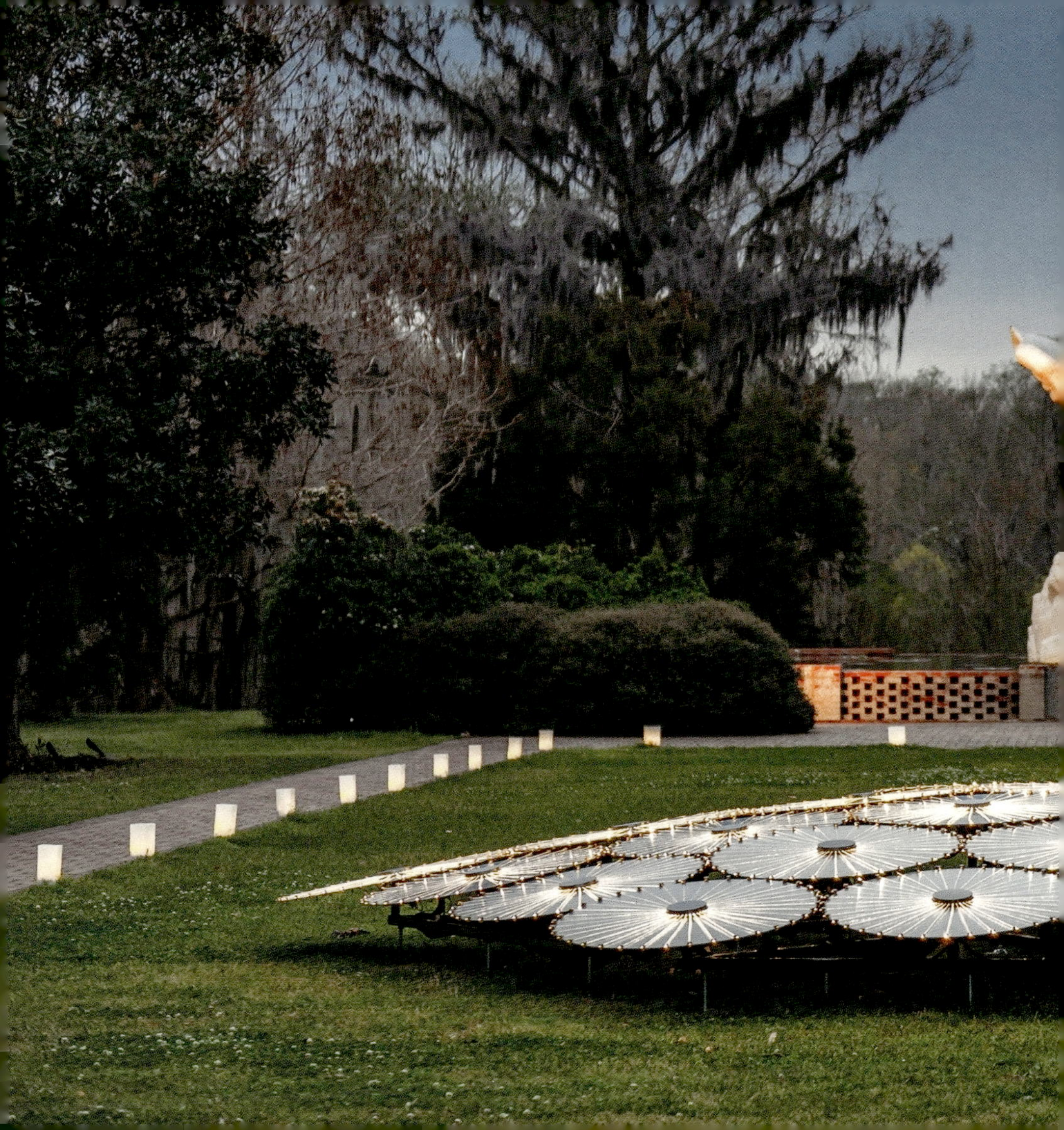

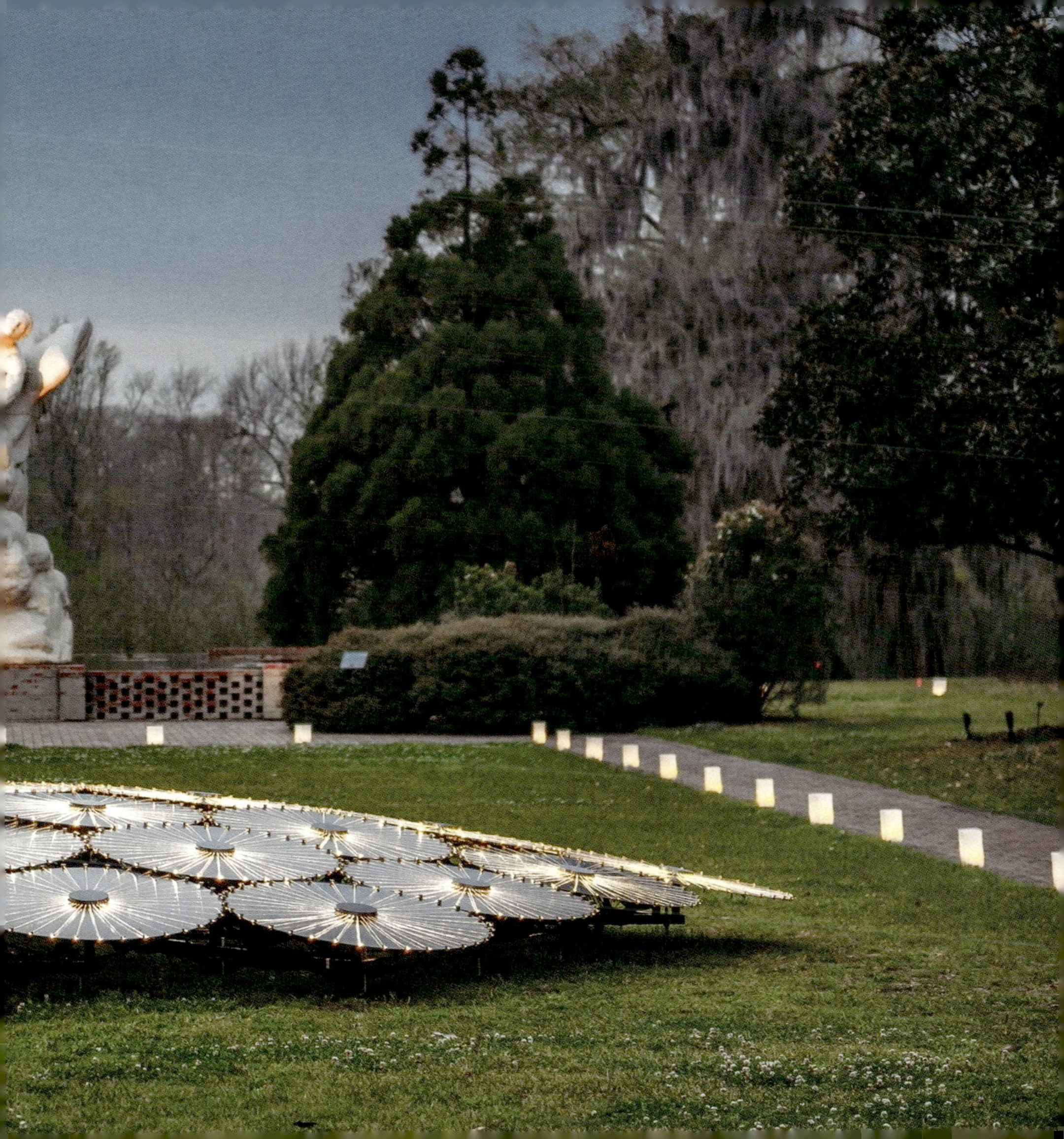

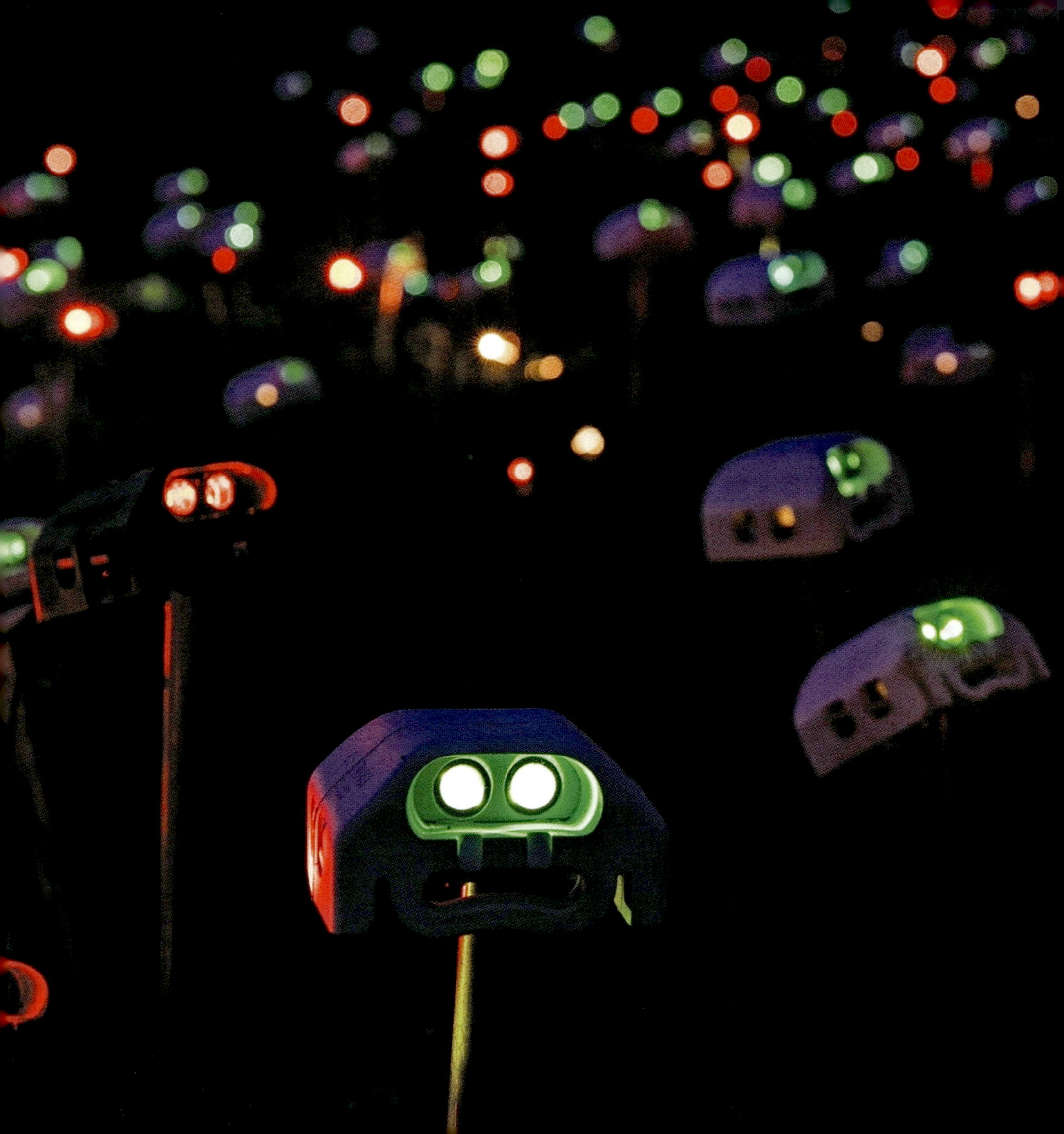

OKONJIMA CHORAL SOCIETY

2020; mixed media (rubber, stainless steel, fiber optics, light, sound)

Okonjima Choral Society was inspired during a family holiday to Okonjima, Namibia, a dedicated wildlife reserve that includes a waterhole that radiates a crescendo of animal sounds at dawn and dusk. The most prominent sound-makers were the indigenous frogs. Three species populated that area, namely, the banded rubber frog, the tremolo sand frog, and the bubbling kassina frog. I developed the concept of an amphibian choir!

Each species of frog in *Okonjima Choral Society* is represented by rubber road-marking inserts and illuminated "eyes." It is accompanied by a program that interprets the sounds of the frogs into pulses and rhythms of illumination. The audio-visual synchronization is an important element of the installation.

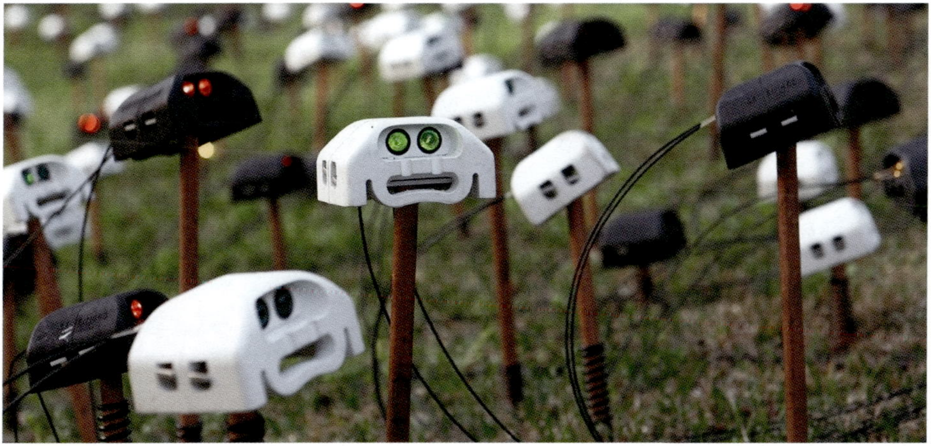

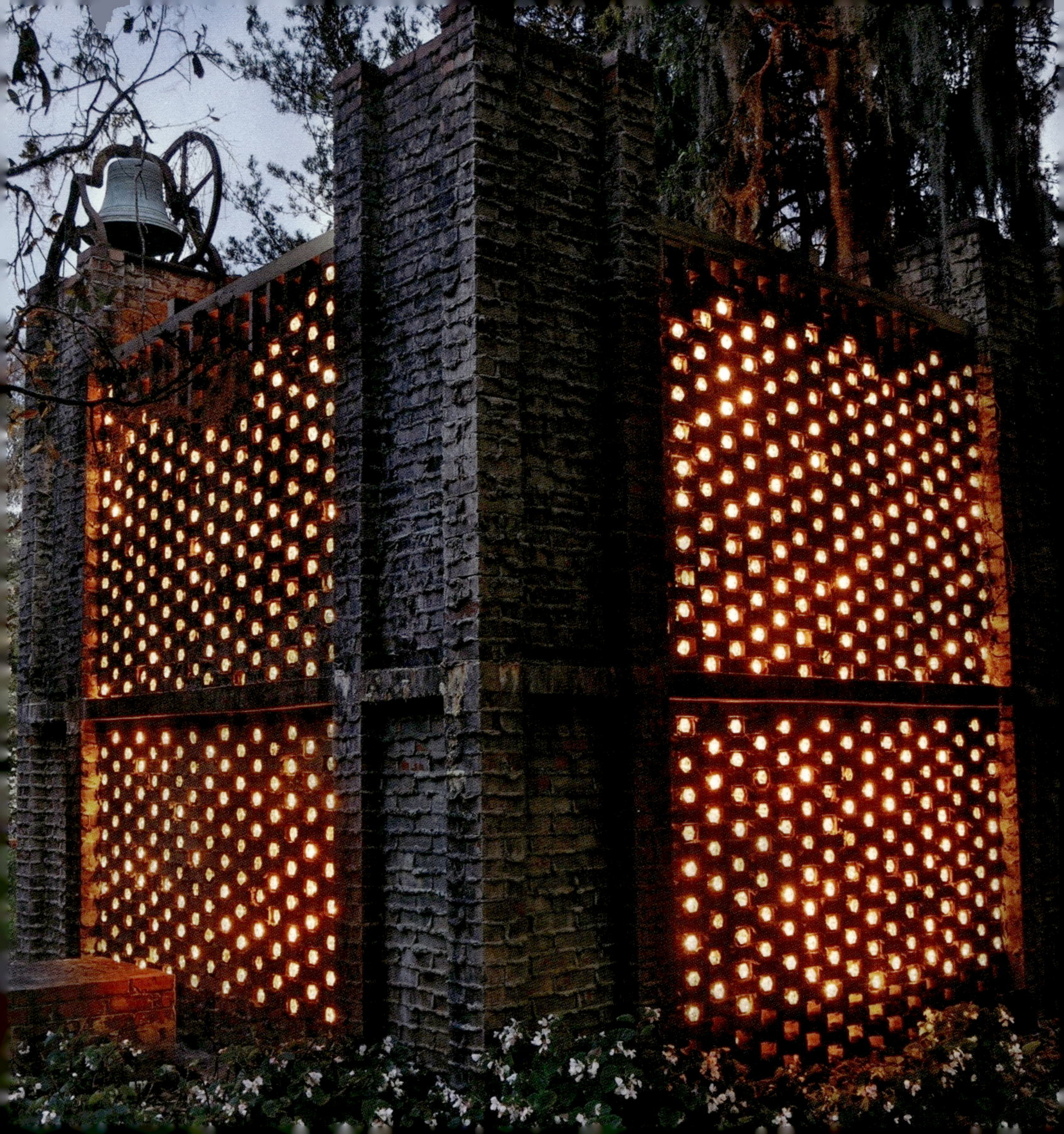

HIVE

2020; mixed media (acrylic, fiber optics, light, sound)

The Bell Tower at Brookgreen Gardens is an architectural feature shrouded by foliage and dappled light. The simple construction, a filigree lattice of ancient bricks, for some reason inspired the idea that this was, in fact, a giant beehive designed by man. There is something rather beautiful about the possibility of calling in the bees at dusk with a bell.

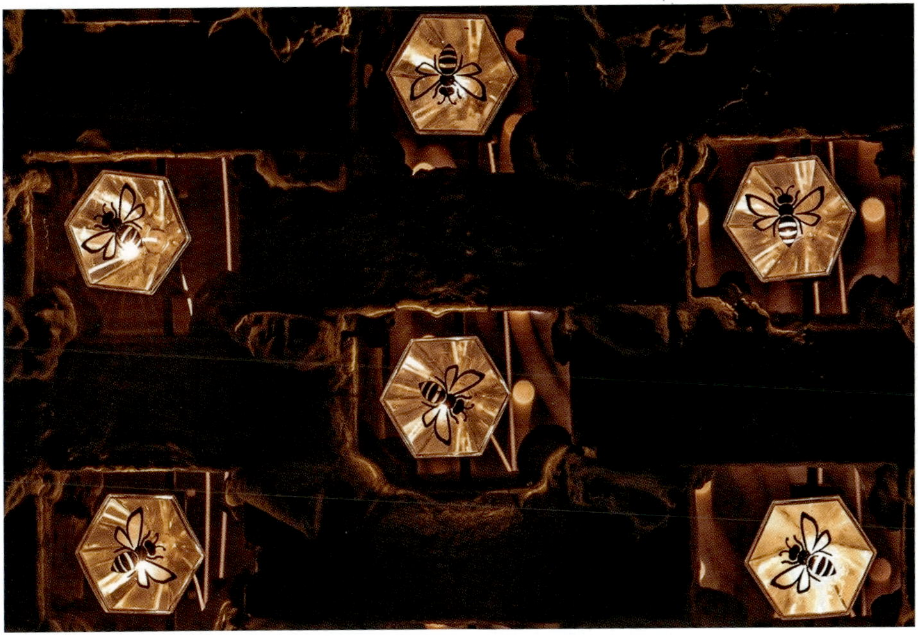

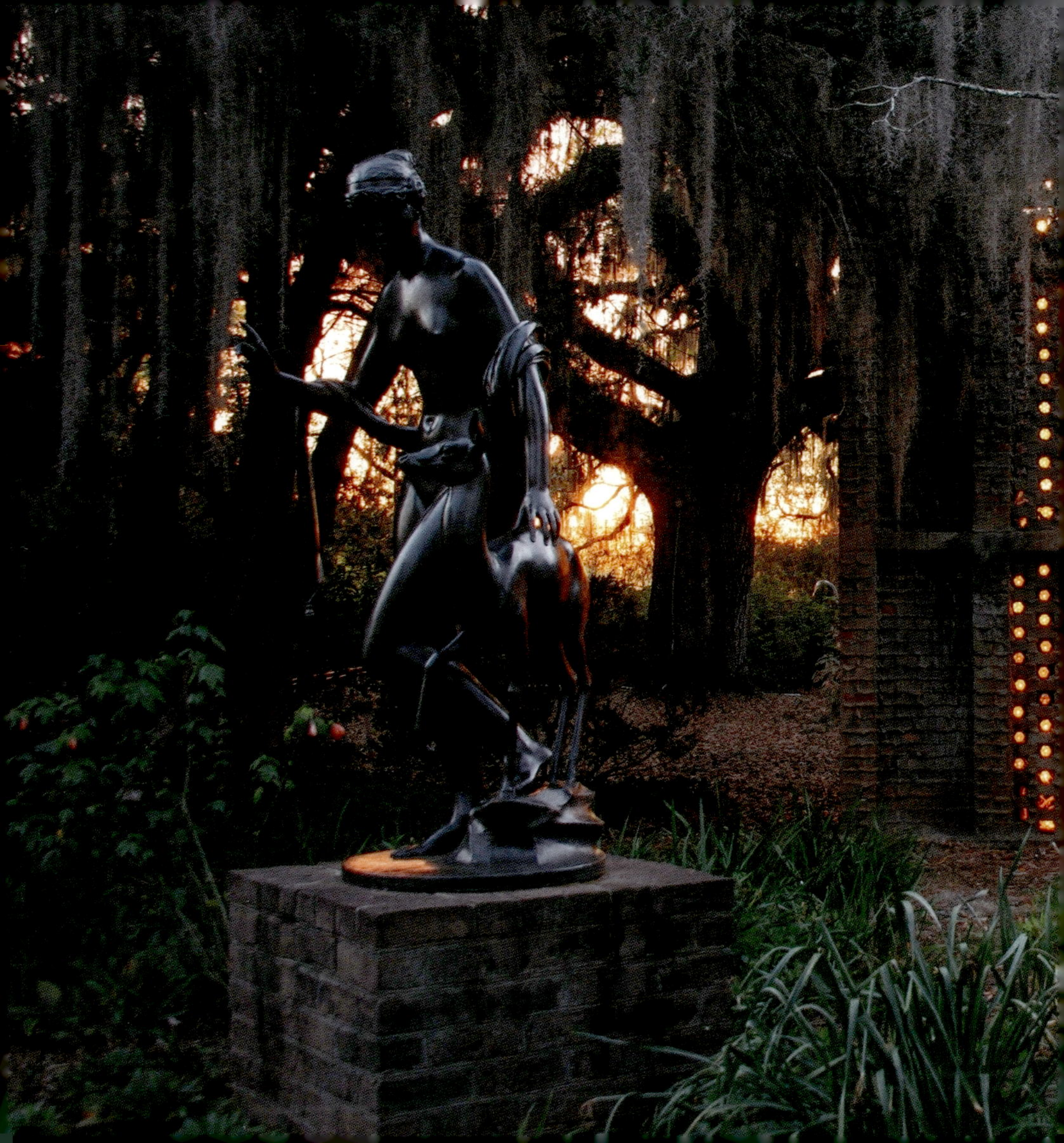

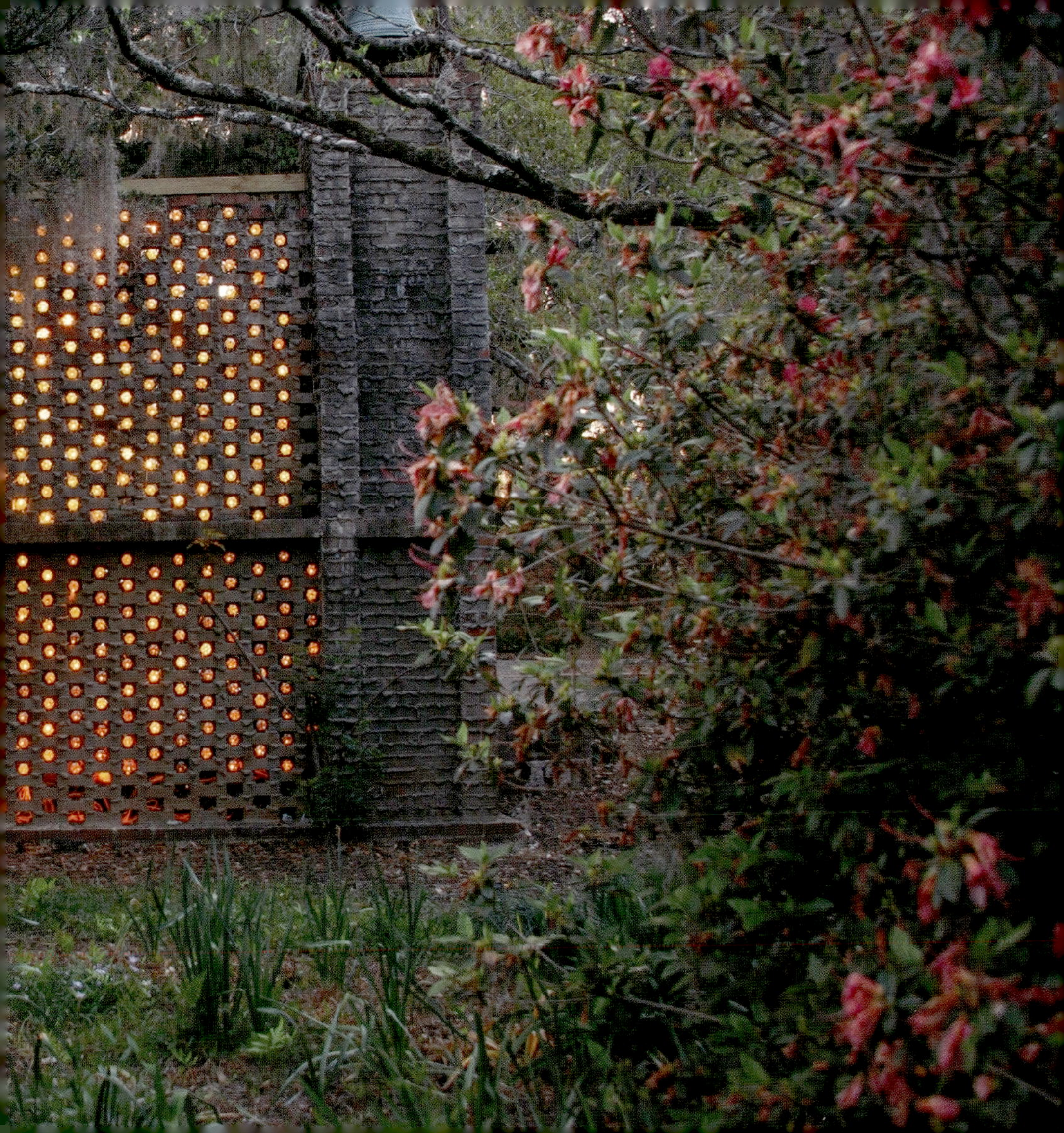

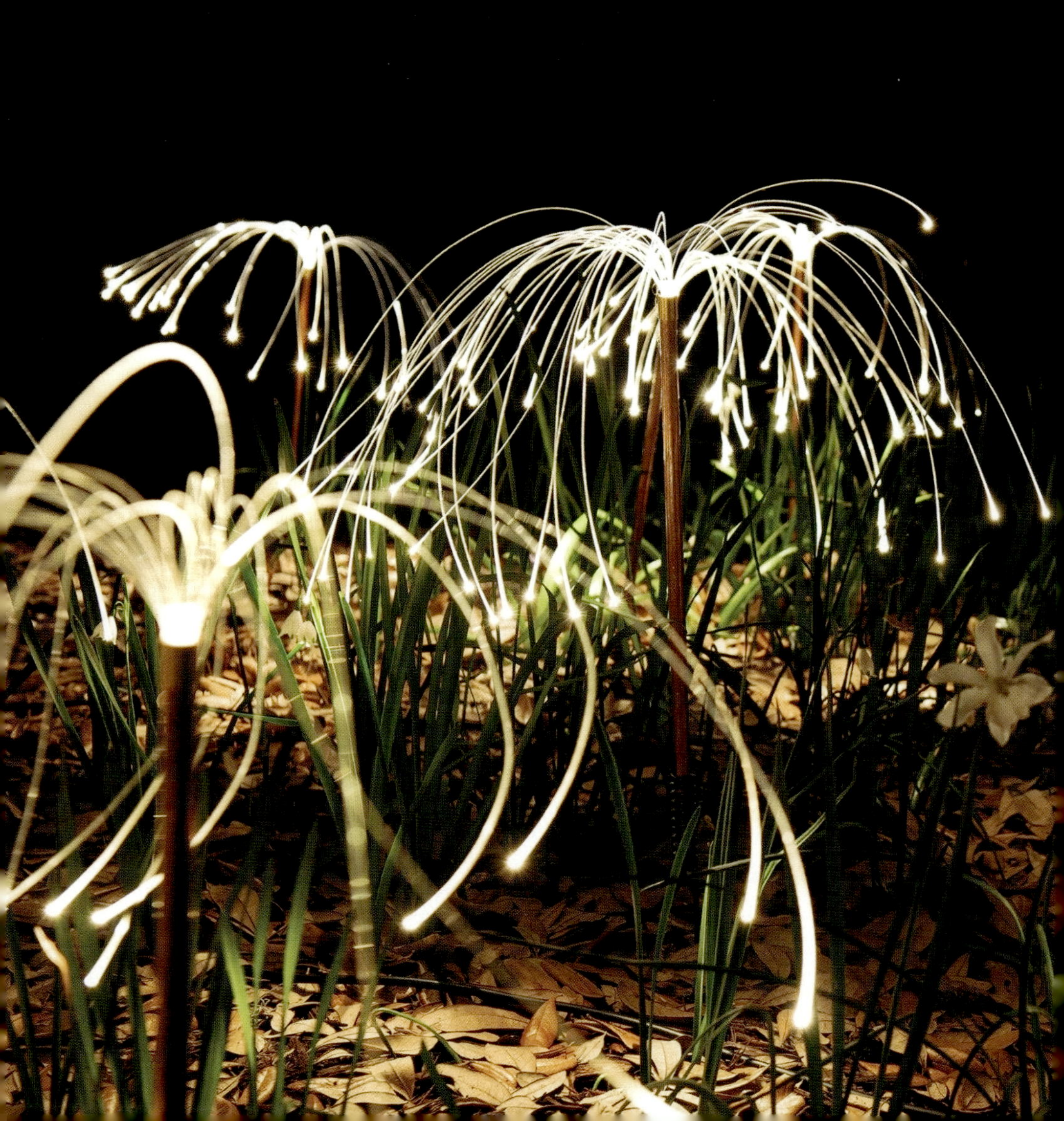

FIREFLIES

2008–2020; mixed media (copper, fiber optics, light source)

I first came up with the form of the *Fireflies* for a residential commission in 2008. Then the idea to develop the piece further came to me on a bike ride in 2010, when I realized there was a personal connection with the spiritual river described in two of my favorite books, *Kim* by Rudyard Kipling and *Siddhartha* by Hermann Hesse.

What I wanted to make was a meandering spring/stream of light, illuminated gently. I began to use the unit form of these individual lovely illuminated objects to create larger site-specific light installations.

For Brookgreen Gardens, I have had the unique opportunity to place them beneath an allée of magnificent and ancient live oak trees. I have found that their repetition and massing can promote a sense of empathy and well-being.

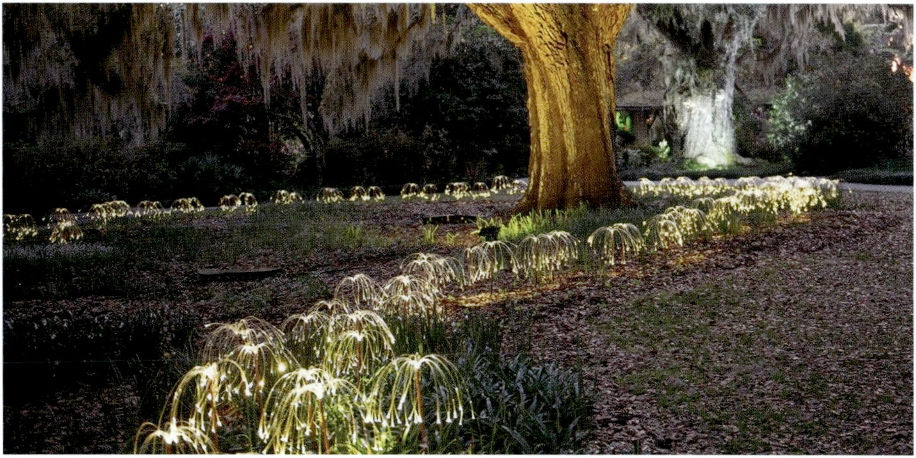

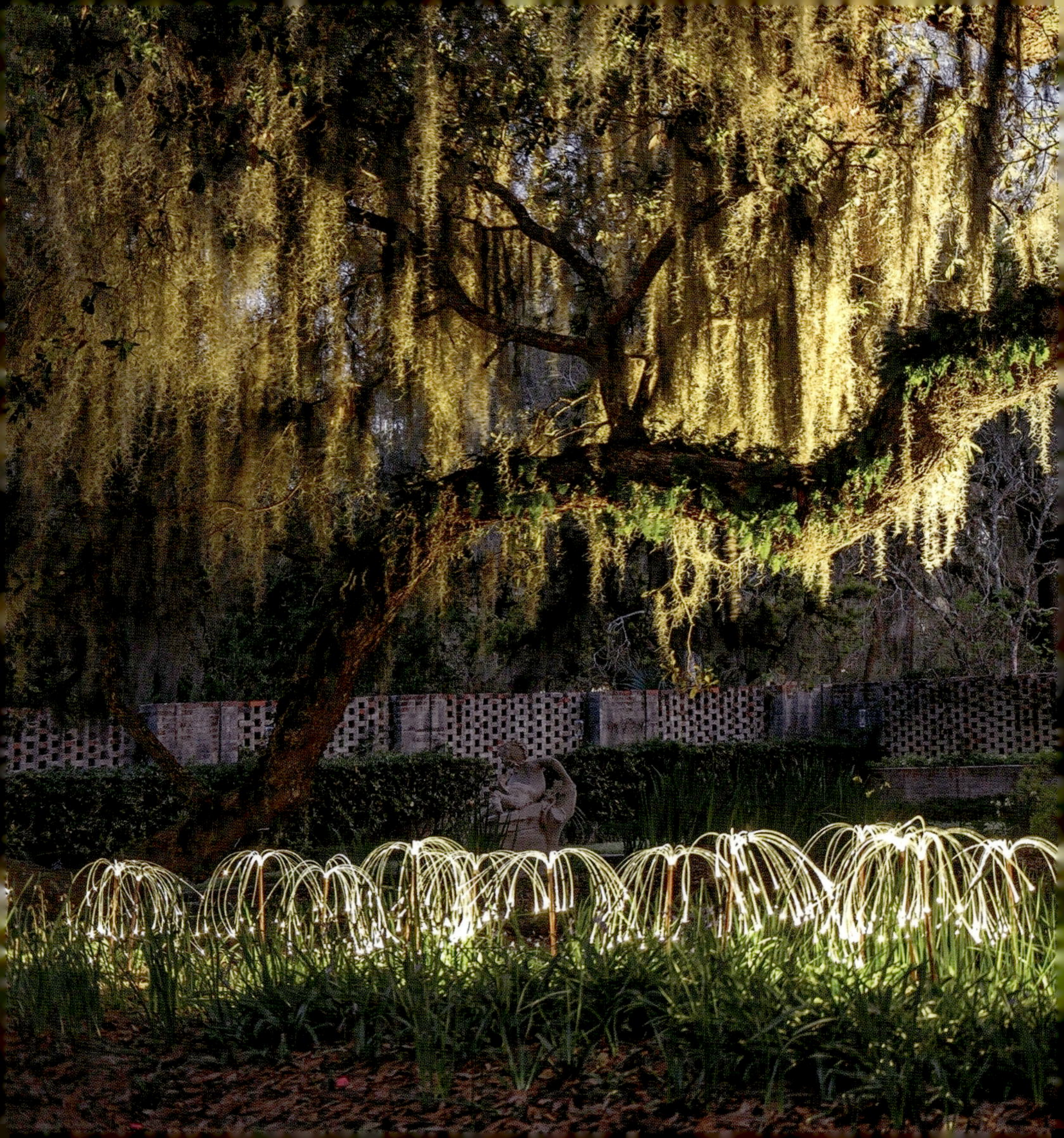

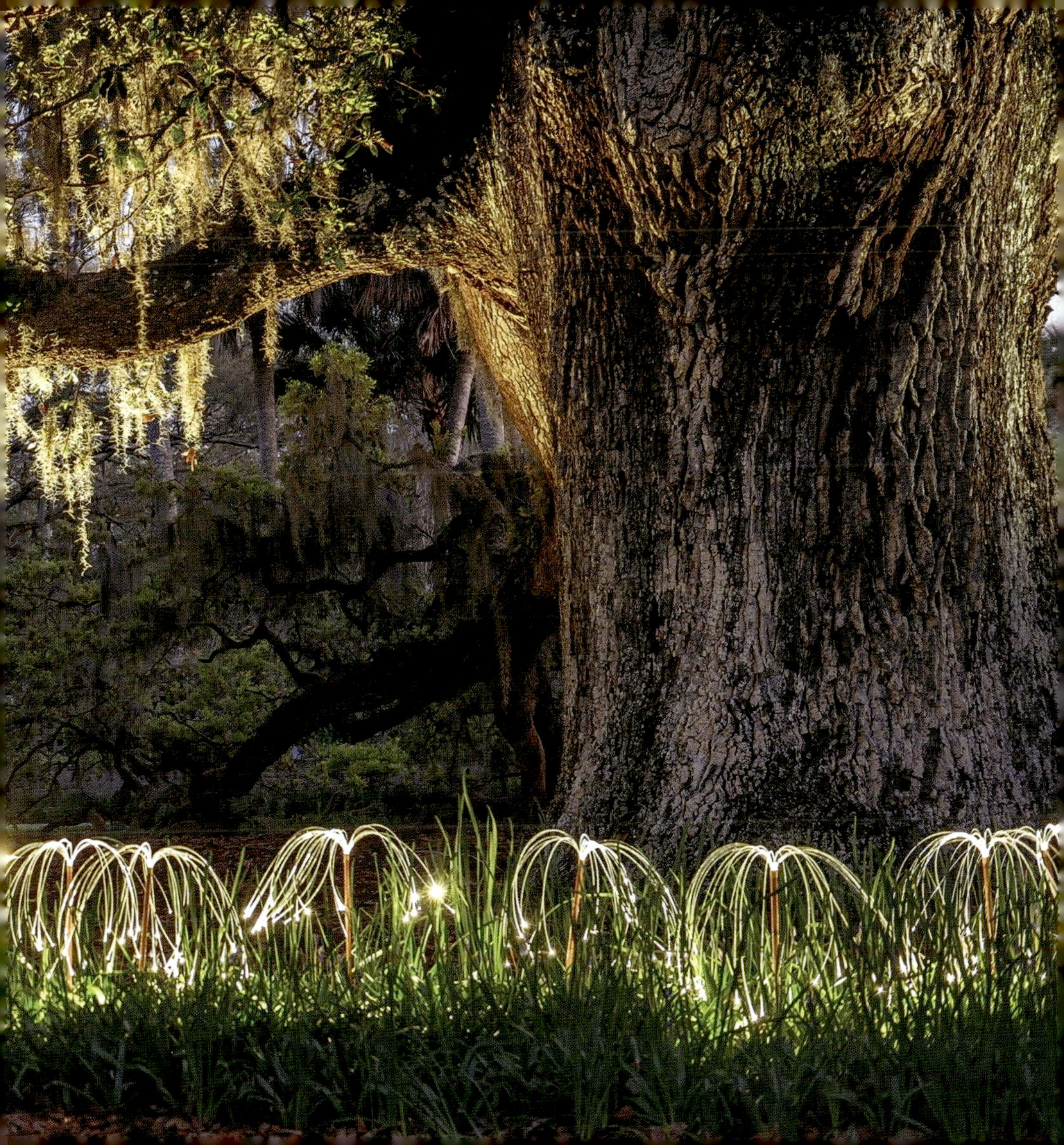

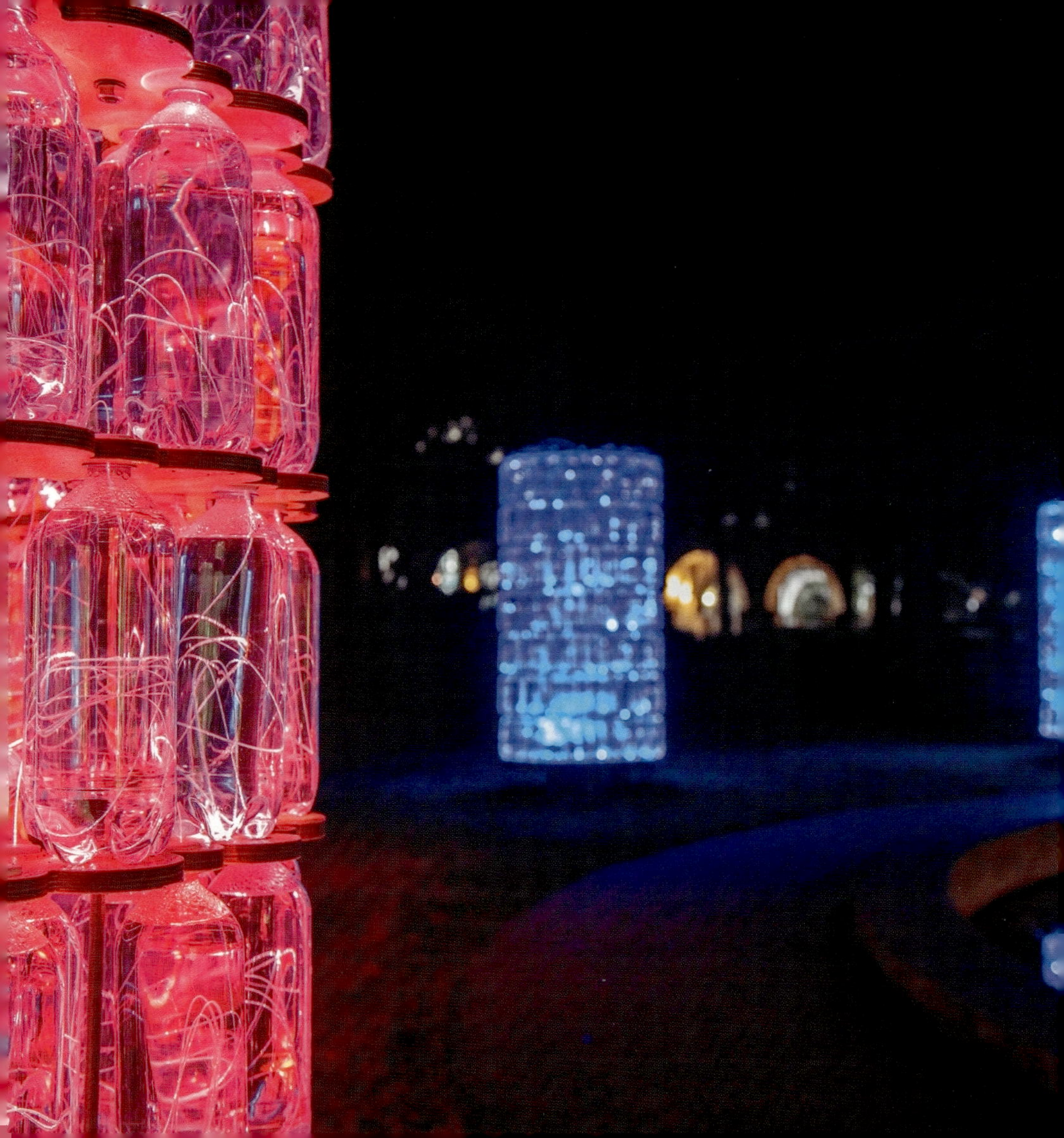

WATER-TOWERS

2012–2020; mixed media (plywood, stainless steel, PET recyclable bottles, fiber optics, light source)

Ten Water-Towers are created from more than 2,500 water-filled one-liter recyclable plastic bottles, each illuminated with optic fibers connected to light projectors and music via audio systems. Each tower responds to the music it "hears," translating that sound into a changing rhythm of colorful light.

I was inspired to create *Water-Towers* after reading a book called *Gifts of Unknown Things*, written by Lyall Watson. The installation is an exercise in creating something magical from simple materials.

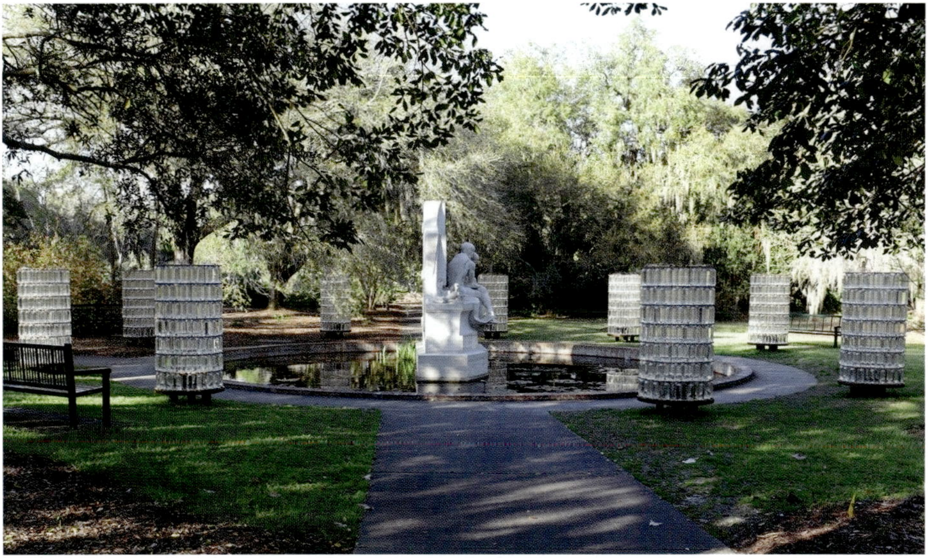

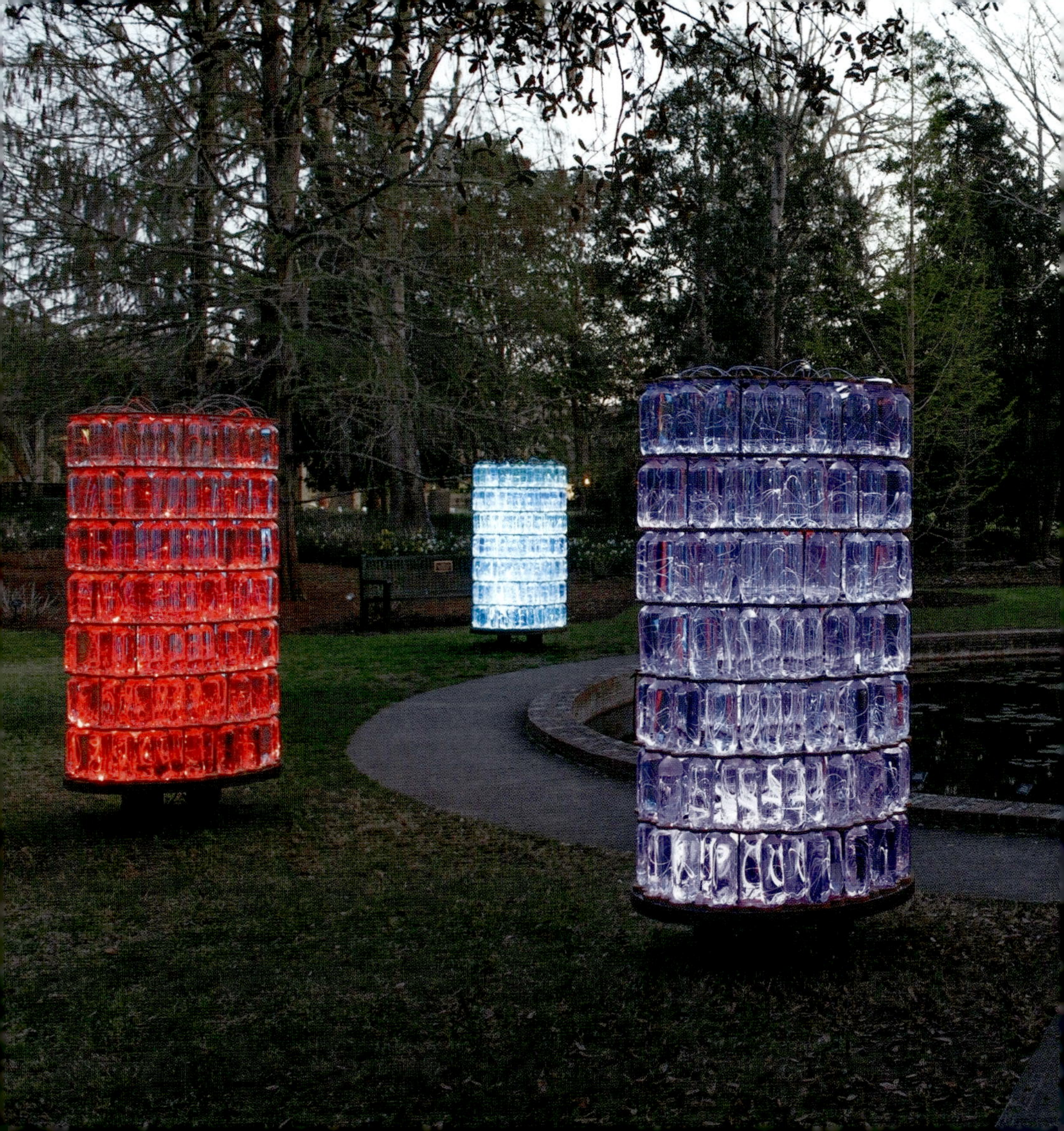

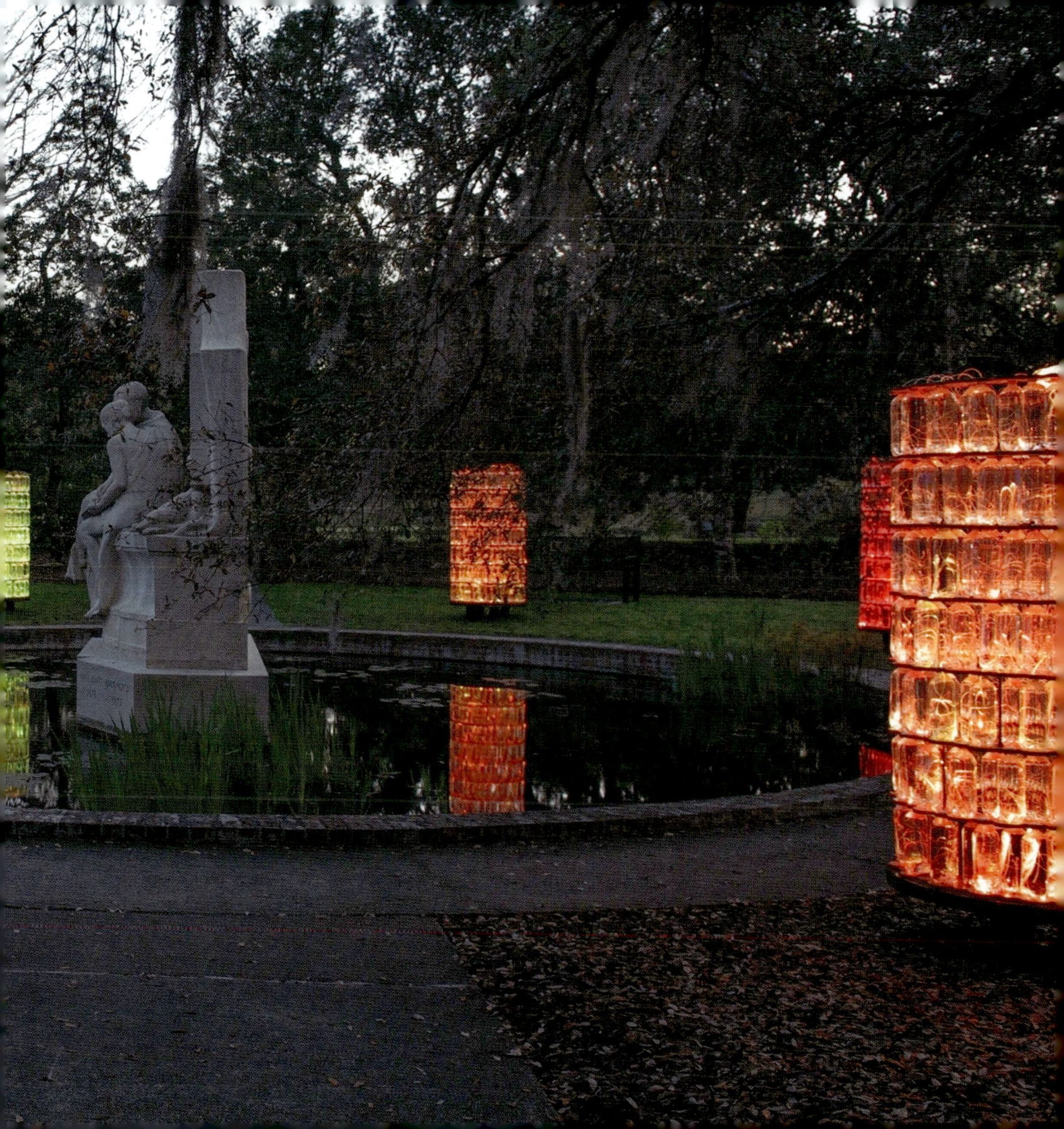

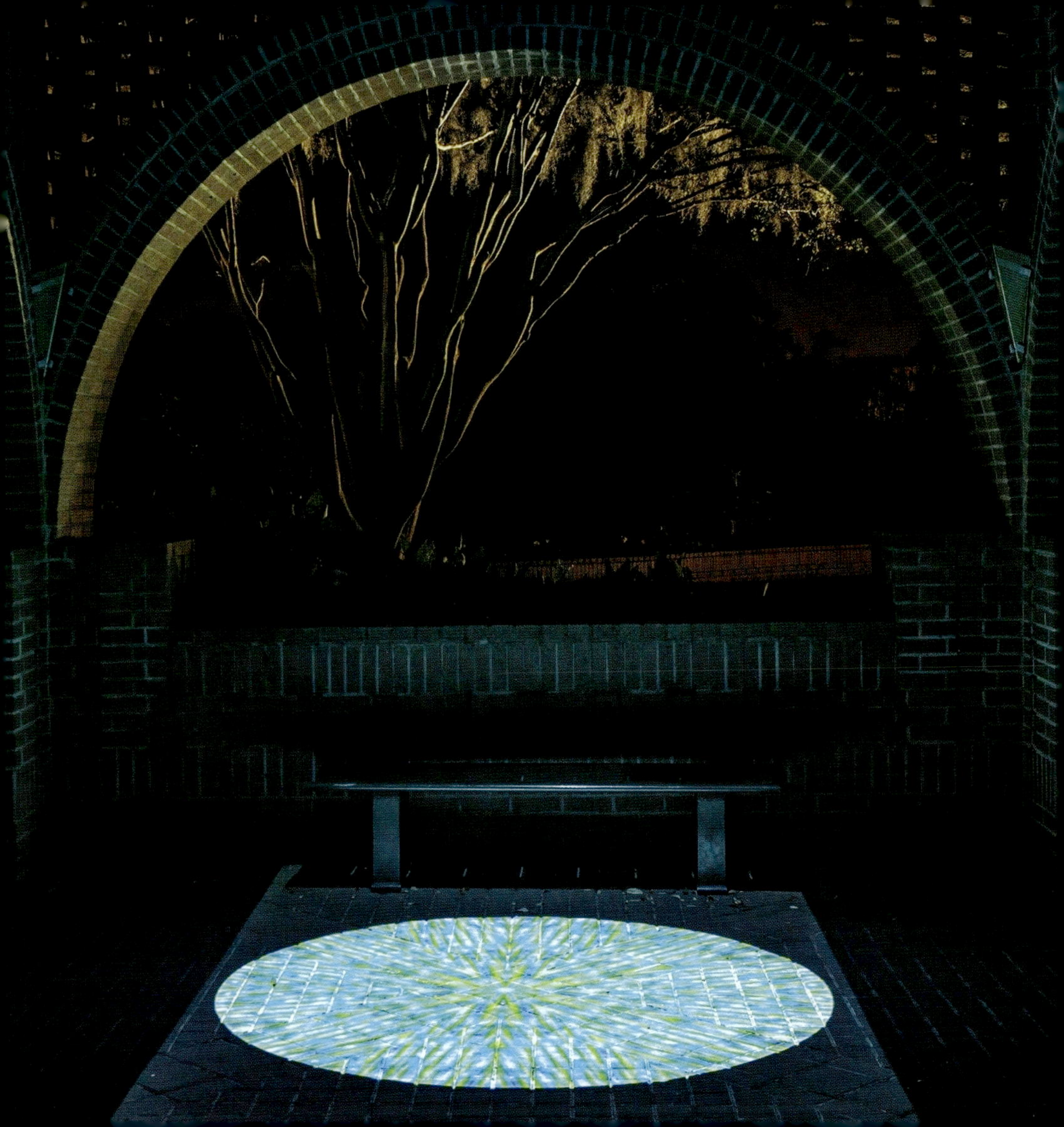

REFLECTIONS

2018–2020; mixed media (animation, low-voltage LED light projection)

In 2013, I began incorporating the communication system of Morse code into digital light animations. Morse code visually reduces an alphabet into dots and dashes of light, allowing me to embed words, equations, and phrases—all decipherable, but also experienced as pattern and movement.

Reflections cycles through four animations, an illuminated carpet of morphing pattern. The first two are Between Worlds—based on the "world between worlds" in C. S. Lewis's Narnian tale *The Magician's Nephew;* and Clouds—which pays homage to William Wordsworth's poem "I Wandered Lonely as a Cloud" and incorporates the chemical equation for photosynthesis translated into Morse code. The final two, Anahata and Nam-Myoho-Renge-Kyo, are based on Buddhist meditation exercises.

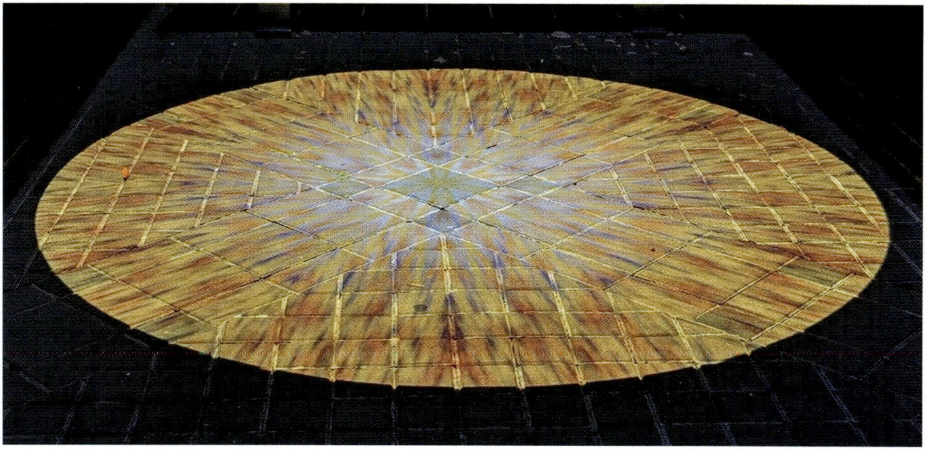

To my wife, Serena

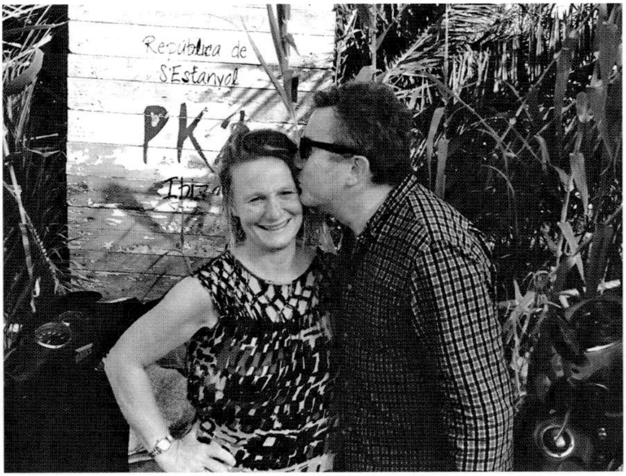

BIOGRAPHY

British artist Bruce Munro is best known for producing large, immersive, light-based installations, which often employ a massing of components by the thousands. An artistic diarist, he has spent over thirty years collecting and recording ideas and images in his sketchbooks, to which he returns over time for source material. Frequently, Munro's subject matter is his own experience of fleeting moments of rapport with the world and existence in its largest sense—of being part of life's essential pattern. His reoccurring motif is the use of light on an environmental scale in order to evoke an emotional response in the viewer.

Born in London in 1959, Munro completed a B.A. in Fine Arts at Bristol in 1982. Shortly thereafter, he moved to Sydney, where he took up employment in design and lighting, inspired by Australia's natural light and landscape. Returning to England in 1992, he settled in Wiltshire, where he and his wife raised four children. Following his father's death in 1999, Munro felt compelled to resume artmaking on a personal level.

His work has been shown at the Victoria & Albert Museum, London; Waddesdon Manor, the Rothschild Collection, Buckinghamshire; and the Guggenheim Museum, New York. Artworks by Munro are held in museum and public collections internationally, including the Ashmolean Museum, Oxford.

In 2016, Munro, supported by Australia's Indigenous Land Corporation, mounted *Field of Light: Uluṟu*, at the place that had first inspired it in 1992, fulfilling a dream of almost twenty-five years. The Uluṟu installation will remain in place throughout 2020.